Vielen Dank für

Deinen Beitrag

Frankfurt, den 18.11.15

Business Intelligence for New-Generation Managers

Jörg H. Mayer • Reiner Quick
Editors

Business Intelligence for New-Generation Managers

Current Avenues of Development

Springer

Editors
Jörg H. Mayer
School of Management
University of St. Gallen
St. Gallen
Switzerland

Reiner Quick
Chair of Accounting and Auditing
Darmstadt University of Technology
Darmstadt
Germany

ISBN 978-3-319-15695-8 ISBN 978-3-319-15696-5 (eBook)
DOI 10.1007/978-3-319-15696-5

Library of Congress Control Number: 2015937247

Springer Cham Heidelberg New York Dordrecht London

Printed on acid-free paper

Springer International Publishing AG Switzerland is part of Springer Science+Business Media (www.springer.com)

Editorial

Business Intelligence for New-Generation Managers: Current Avenues of Development

Taking the 2008/2009 economic crisis and the ongoing financial turbulences as a reference point, companies have to operate in an increasingly dynamic environment [2]. This has not just led to a significant development from pure financial accounting to a plurality of corporate management ideas [7], but in managers' information system (IS) design as well [4].

Business intelligence (BI) plays an important role in such an IS design as BI is designed to be managers' central, hands-on, and day-to-day valuable information source [3]. BI should provide the right information with the right quality and at the right time from different internal and external data sources [1].

Based on Wixom and Watson [9], we define *BI for managers* as a broad category of applications, technologies, and processes for gathering, storing, accessing, and analyzing data to help such managers to make better decisions. Following a "typical" decision-making process [8], this Springer contributed volume on BI for new-generation managers outlines avenues of development of their information need analysis (A), information collection (B), and information synthesis and presentation (C) [5].

(A) Starting with managers' *information need analysis*, they have expanded their role in operations—parallel to their strategic leadership. At the same time, they have to make decisions faster than in the past [6]. The first chapter "*On the Advent of Operational Perspectives in Business Intelligence*" by Tom Hänel analyzes BI in terms of supporting operational and strategic decision. One of his findings is that operational BI design requires higher data accuracy and a much greater amount of details. The holistic establishment of BI on all levels of operative decisions enables an exact measurement of efficiency and therefore connects the operational level directly to strategic ones.

Complementing these findings with a perspective on strategic decision making, Claudia Koschtial and Carsten Felden reflect with their chapter "*On the Way from a Knowledge Discovery in Databases to a Predictive Analytics*" such decisions and their BI support. Their approach is about knowledge discovery in databases to improve forecast quality. Environmental Scanning Systems fit into this direction of prediction as well. Using the KDD markup language, they enhance analyzed data with additional future-oriented data. Hence forecasting stops to predict the past but improves its precision.

Performance measurement systems are another approach of consolidating data in a compact yet comprehensive way according to managers' information needs. Maurice Kügler and Christoph Nowakowski, in their chapter "*Design and Implementation of a Performance Measurement System for the German Trade Sector*", propose a performance measurement system adjusted to managers' trade sector-specific information needs. The authors develop a straightforward approach for calculating and visualizing an organization's key performance indicators and reports on its implementation in a BI environment. The content on this chapter is part of a research project which was awarded the EHI Research Award from EHI Retail Institute.

The chapter "*Applicability of Environmental Scanning Systems: A Systematic List Approach to Requirements Criteria*" by Stefan Bischoff, Timm Weitzel, Jörg H. Mayer, and Reiner Quick complements this avenue of BI development for strategic decision making. The authors develop a systematic list approach to requirements criteria that specify the applicability of such IS. The criteria are derived from the principle of economic efficiency and can be applied to both evaluate existing environmental scanning systems and develop a new, more applicable generation.

(B) An organization has always to deal with the challenge how much information is needed for decision making and how this information has to be customized to company-specific requirements per se and especially managers' way to make decisions. Thus, *collecting the "right" data* for managers' decision making strongly determines the cost/benefit ratio of IS. Janusch Patas addresses this research topic by developing a method to systematically adjust maturity models (MMs) from the knowledge base to firm-specific business needs. In his chapter "*Developing individual IT-Enabled Capabilities for Management Control Systems*," he presents a list of IT and non-IT assets that are necessary for companies to develop individual IT-enabled planning and reporting capabilities. Practice will benefit from an individual view on their IT-enabled capabilities and it forces managers to jointly consider their IT and non-IT assets when they are designing IT-enabled capabilities for their company.

The chapter "*Towards an Evaluation Framework to Structure Business Intelligence Project Patterns as Enhancement of Business Intelligence Maturity Models*" by Carsten Felden, Claudia Koschtial, and Peter Chamoni examines BI project descriptions which were part of the German TDWI "Best Paper Award" to examine pattern for "typical" BI project definitions. In doing so, they differentiate between technology, organization, and business environment. The framework derived from 45 analyzed projects helps to find a company's benchmark in relation to others in comparison to an elaborate process analysis which would be needed to find a reference point in a maturity model.

Big data is another emerging research topic in information collection. The term remains fuzzy and jeopardizes to become an umbrella term. The chapter "*Descriptive Big Data Model Using Grounded Theory*" by Marco Pospiech and Carsten Felden executes expert interviews to identify a common understanding. The outcome is a model which enables to classify and clarify big data contents and herewith separating buzz wording from progress.

(C) A misalignment in *information synthesis and presentation* often exposes difficulties that IT departments face to meet expectations of their business counterparts. The chapter "*Business Intelligence 2.0*" by Sebastian Behrendt and Alexander Richter discusses new ways of analyzing data. Bearing in mind changing communication and joint work, they focus on the growing importance of Enterprise Social Networks. The authors end with a proposal for a method mix for practice.

Last but not least, creating a new management support system, Jörg H. Mayer, Jens Hartwig, André Röder, and Reiner Quick derive in their chapter "*Self-Service Management Support Systems: Findings from a New-Generation Manager Perspective*" a set of business-driven design guidelines from the findings of a multi-case study within German DAX companies. The utility of these guidelines is demonstrated with a "mobile-first" prototype on a modern BI platform.

Finally, we would like to thank Markus Eßwein, Darmstadt University of Technology, for coordinating the process of collecting and formatting all the contributions on hand with great patience and care over the last 6 months.

St.Gallen, Switzerland — Jörg H. Mayer
Darmstadt, Germany — Reiner Quick

References

1. Anandarajan M, Anandarajan A, Srinivasan CA (2004) Business intelligence techniques. A perspective from accounting and finance. Springer, Berlin
2. Anthony RN, Govindarajan V (2007) Management control systems. McGraw-Hill/Irwin, New York
3. Gartner (1996) IT glossary: business intelligence. http://www.gartner.com/it-glossary/business-intelligence-bi. Accessed 10 Oct 2013
4. Marx F, Wortmann F, Mayer JH (2012) A maturity model for management control systems—five evolutionary steps to guide development. Bus Inform Syst Eng 4(4):193–207
5. Mayer JH (1999) Führungsinformationssysteme für die internationale Management-Holding. Gabler, Wiesbaden
6. Mayer JH (2013) Current changes in executive work and how to handle them by redesigning executive information systems. In: Mancini D, Vaassen E, Dameri RP (eds) Accounting information systems for decision making. Springer, Heidelberg, pp 151–173

7. Seal W (2010) Managerial discourse and the link between theory and practice: from ROI to value-based management. Manag Account Res 21(2):95–109
8. Simon HA (1955) A behavioral model of rational choice. Q J Econ 69(1):99–118
9. Wixom BH, Watson HJ (2010) The BI-based organization. Int J Bus Intell Res 1(1):13–28

Contents

On the Advent of Operational Perspectives in Business Intelligence

Tom Hänel

Abstract Business intelligence (BI) supports the decision making according to strategic and operational management tasks. However, there is no systematic classification so that a decision making can be guided by conformable and well understandable BI topics regarding strategic or operational management activities. A literature review is conducted to identify publications on strategic and operational BI. The classification follows a single word and word group analysis supported by text mining. The results present the trends, along with their interpretation, and a discussion of BI in the context of strategic or operational decision making. The findings identify mature BI literature contributing to strategic decision making. The chapter implicates avenues of future research in context of operational management activities.

Keywords BI Support for Operational Management Activities • Literature Review

1 Introduction

BI experiences an increasing importance in academia and practice by its expansion on functionalities, available data sets, and its usage on all organizational layers [5]. This provides decision making capabilities to compete in dynamic and uncertain business environments [40]. A decision maker's focus depends thereby on his/her managerial tasks [19]. Different managerial tasks require a different BI support [29, 34]. A systematic reference in this field of discourse leads to benefits for decision makers' understanding to gain a helpful BI capability and a task-oriented application. An identification of trends is also of scientific interest as it allows an overview of potential research topics. This chapter 's goal is therefore to analyze BI in terms of different management tasks. It provides a literature overview of similarities and differences, as well as development trends.

The characteristics of BI are discussed according to the information needs of decision makers [30, 34]. Currently, there is a discussion of strategic and

T. Hänel (✉)
Technische Universität Bergakademie Freiberg, Freiberg, Germany
e-mail: tom.haenel@bwl.tu-freiberg.de

J.H. Mayer, R. Quick (eds.), *Business Intelligence for New-Generation Managers*,
DOI 10.1007/978-3-319-15696-5_1

operational BI capabilities [6, 43]. Especially investigations on operational BI refer exclusively to practical contributions. Scientific publications use without exceptions white papers or research reports of associations of practitioners regarding to BI (e.g. [8, 10, 41]) to motivate the research. Methods of reviewing literature to detect knowledge gaps in favor of subsequent research actions [39] are not considered in papers on operational BI. Motivations need an observation of BI from a scientific point of view to achieve a comprehensive basis. However, a classification based on strategic and operational management activities does not occur in the literature, yet. Therefore, the chapter contributes to the discussion of BI and information demand-oriented decision making. It provides a literature classification of topics, trends, relationships, and characteristics of strategic and operational BI. It also delivers a structure of relevant findings to avoid duplication efforts in context of subsequent research activities.

Section 2 discusses BI in context of strategic and operational decisions. This includes an analysis of existing reviews of BI to demonstrate the need for further investigations. The chapter uses a phase-oriented approach for a profound literature analysis. Section 3 complements these phases to achieve a resilient classification of BI publications. Section 4 interprets the classification results. A conclusion summarizes the chapter and gives further research perspectives.

2 The Understanding of BI in Context of Data and Their Managerial Usage Level

Starting in 1958, BI was introduced to support a decision making in organizations. Luhn discussed the general need of understanding managerial situations to achieve goal-oriented actions [25]. Despite this early appearance of BI it is still challenging to find a unique and accepted definition of BI so that for example Hugh Watson pursues a broad definition of BI instead [36]:

> Business intelligence (BI) is a broad category of applications, technologies, and processes for gathering, storing, accessing, and analyzing data to help business users make better decisions.

This definition focuses on aspects of loading data into a data warehouse and retrieving data out of a data warehouse for decision making [38]. Such a broad classification is also evident in the literature reviews (cf. Table 1).

However, even broad BI perspectives ignore the discussion that a BI support depends on the information needs of business users according to their certain management task [30, 34]. There is a differentiation between strategic and operational BI capabilities [6]. The intersection of BI and strategic decisions deals with organizational performance issues and market orientation to gain competitive advantages or to consolidate a market position [43]. An application of BI techniques within processes is subject of operational BI capabilities [26]. They pursue timely and fast reactions or forecasts to current business situations [43]. Both BI capabilities lead to business value, i.e. a competitive advantage in favor of strategic

Table 1 Literature reviews of BI

Source	Summary
[33]	BI gathers, stores, and analyzes data to produce information and knowledge for purposive decisions. Associated technologies are data warehousing, OLAP, knowledge management systems and decision support systems
[20]	BI can be classified into five distinct categories: artificial intelligence, usage to achieve financial benefits, improvement of overall decision making, BI project management issues and application strategies for BI tools and technologies
[5]	BI considers structured, unstructured, as well as mobile and sensor based content. The applications are manifold including e-commerce and market intelligence, e-government and politics 2.0, science and technology, smart health and wellbeing, security and public safety. Emerging research is suggested for big data analytics, text analytics, web analytics, network analytics, and mobile analytics

Table 2 Information requirements according to [11]

	Operational	Strategic
Source	Internal	External
Scope	Defined, narrow	Wide
Level of aggregation	Detailed	Aggregate
Time horizon	Historical	Future
Currency	Current	Old
Required accuracy	High	Low
Frequency of use	Frequent	Infrequent

goals based on internal process improvements in an operational context [32]. Strategic BI capabilities have to be understood as prerequisite for operational BI capabilities [26]. Gorry and Morton [11] provide a detailed classification on the information requirements of strategic and operational management tasks (cf. Table 2).

Strategic information encompasses a wide content and timeline scope and stems rather from external sources. They are usually available on an aggregated level. The demand of strategic information is sporadic and future-oriented. Operational information use is frequent requiring high accuracy and currency on a detailed level of aggregation. Their focus is on reaction of occurrences in a defined scope using primarily internal sources [11].

Hayen [14] for example investigates 48 case study publications of BI applications in context of operational and strategic management levels. The analysis uses the information requirements according to Gorry and Morton [11] (cf. Table 3).

The applied framework emphasizes on scope, level of aggregation, and frequency of use. Characteristics concerning the range of users, operational efficiency, the duration of use, and the need for rapid developments are added. Hayen's findings do not provide insights about development trends of strategic or operational BI. There is also no assignment of business applications to these categories.

Table 3 Adapted information requirements of BI [14]

	Operational	Strategic
Scope	Defined, narrow	Wide
Level of aggregation	Detailed	Aggregate
Required accuracy	High	Low
Frequency of use	Frequent	Infrequent
Range of user	Wide	Narrow
Operational efficiency	High	Low
Duration of use	Long	Short
Rapid development need	Low	High

Furthermore, a rigorous literature review method is missing so that the case selection is hardly comprehensible.

The discussion demonstrates that the literature is insufficient to apply a conjoint review of BI applications in a strategic or operational context. Considering the circumstances that strategic and operational BI capabilities create business value [32], an analysis is needed to describe fields of BI applications and their characteristics. This is beneficial to consolidate the scientific knowledge regarding meaning and trends of BI in the area of strategic or operational decisions.

3 Method

The method follows a common phase-oriented approach [7]. A literature search considers the scientific databases of Business Source Complete (BSC), IEEE Xplore, AIS electronic Library (AISeL), ACM Digital Library, Emerald and Science Direct (SD). The search term is "Business Intelligence". Its appearance is limited to abstract, title, or keywords. The date of publication is not later than March 31, 2013. The search leads to an initial data set of 1,322 publications.

A group of two researchers evaluated all papers against the demonstrated understanding of BI. Papers using BI just as an abstract label for business knowledge and know-how were excluded. The researchers classified the papers using Hayen's information requirements and situational characteristics [14]. The evaluation reveals 1,057 publications classified in strategic and operational BI. The first category is also used for papers understanding BI as a holistic concept for an interrelated management of strategic and operational management levels. Each paper was also assigned to an industry and a functional application.

4 Results

The results encompass 537 papers on strategic BI and 520 papers on operational BI. Figure 1 illustrates the chronology of both categories.

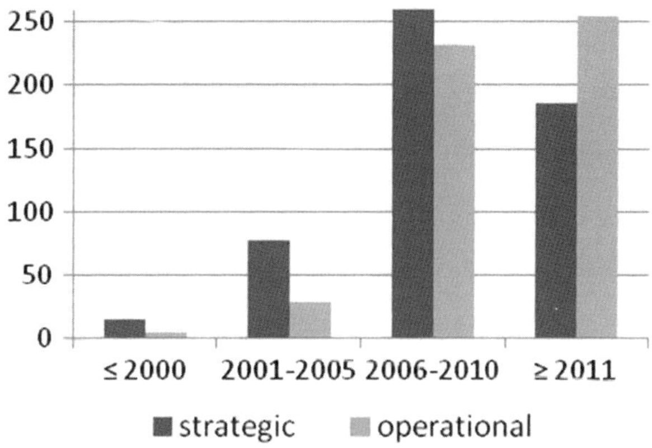

Fig. 1 Chronology of investigated papers

The results are described and analyzed in context of industries and functional application areas. This chapter presents subsequently a text mining analysis based on the programming language *R* [44]. This approach pursues an evaluation of the classification's quality and resilience, and allows a content interpretation. However, the results are not a random sample of practical BI implementations. They reflect the relation of strategic and operational management to BI from a scientific point of view.

4.1 Analysis by Application Areas

The classification's industry profile consists of ten specific and one overarching group (cf. Fig. 2).

A majority of papers on strategic and operational BI is cross industry with an ascending trend to strategic considerations. These papers could not be assigned to any distinct industry as none could be defined or they included several different industries at once. The papers on operational BI exceed the papers on strategic BI by 1.5 % in context of trade and service. The relation of BI and strategic decisions is more pronounced in health care, public administration as well as finance, banking, and insurance. The papers on operational BI are focusing to a larger extent on manufacturing, utility companies, education and research, transport as well as information and communications technology (ICT). Small and medium sized companies are likewise addressed in the papers.

Figure 3 shows industry trends presented by papers divided into two different groups by their publication date . The two-section scale is chosen for reasons of readability. The year 2009 serves as split criterion, because there is the most balanced number of the publications. The ratio of papers on operational BI has increased for all industry groups. The focus has changed in seven of eleven groups.

Next to the industry groups, we defined a functional category for each paper (cf. Fig. 4).

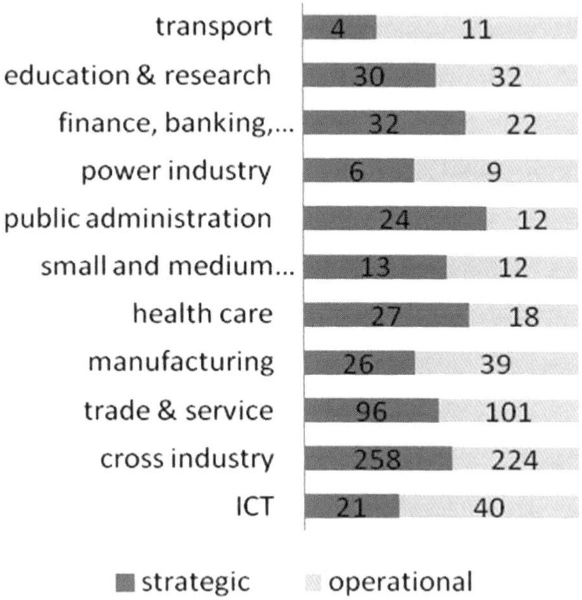

Fig. 2 Industries profile of investigated papers

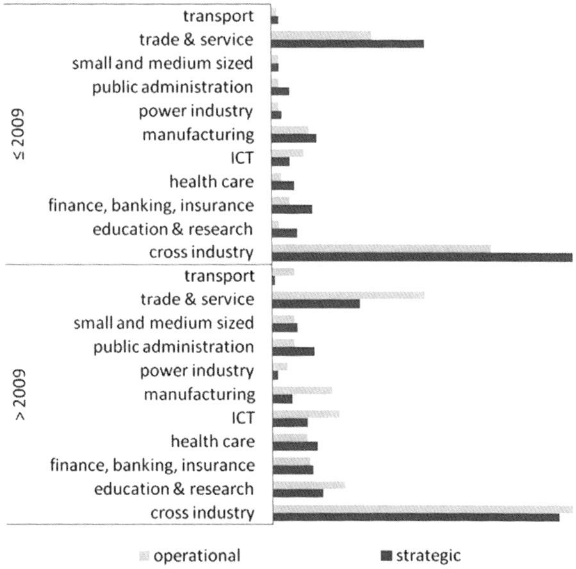

Fig. 3 Industry trend of investigated papers

Architecture and technology aspects characterize investigations on operational BI, while activities of organizational structure and control dominate the papers on strategic BI. The papers on operational BI emphasize more on logistics. Marketing and sales as well as accounting and finance are fairly uniform distributed in comparison to the papers on strategic and operational BI.

Fig. 4 Functional profile of investigated papers

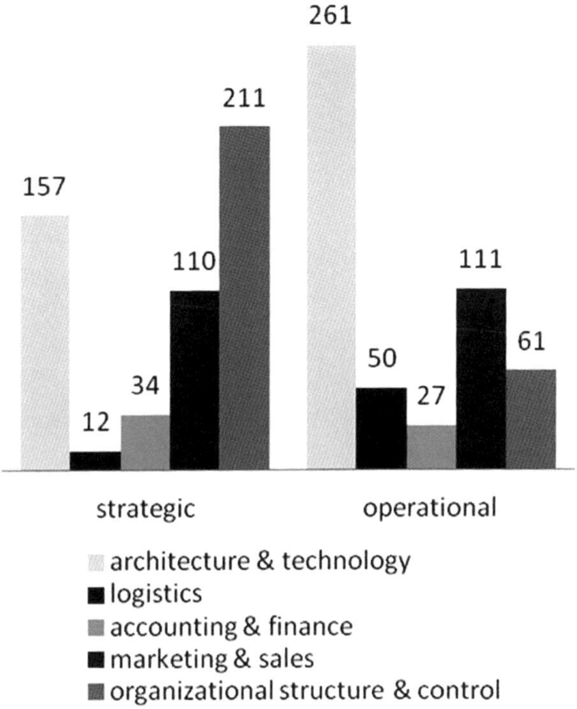

Figure 5 illustrates functional trends using again 2009 as split criterion for a two-section time scale. All functional classes have become more operational and the focus of marketing and sales changed in favor of an operational decision background.

4.2 Analysis by Text Mining

We retrieved the data separately und built two different collections of the papers' abstracts on strategic and operational BI. Every corpus uses the corresponding paper abstracts as vector source. A following text transformation converts the retrieved text elements to lower cases and removed punctuations, numbers, URLs, and stop words. The stop words include a common list of general English terms and an additional list of ca. 200 words considering usual verbs and nouns of abstract writing. A stemming finished the data preprocessing.

Subsequently , we calculated the term frequencies for each data set. Word clouds illustrate the importance of the top 50 terms within the papers' abstracts on strategic and operational BI. The terms *data*, *business*, *intelligence*, and *system* are discarded for reasons of readability and clarity, because these are the most frequent words in the papers' abstracts on strategic and operational BI. Figure 6 illustrates the word

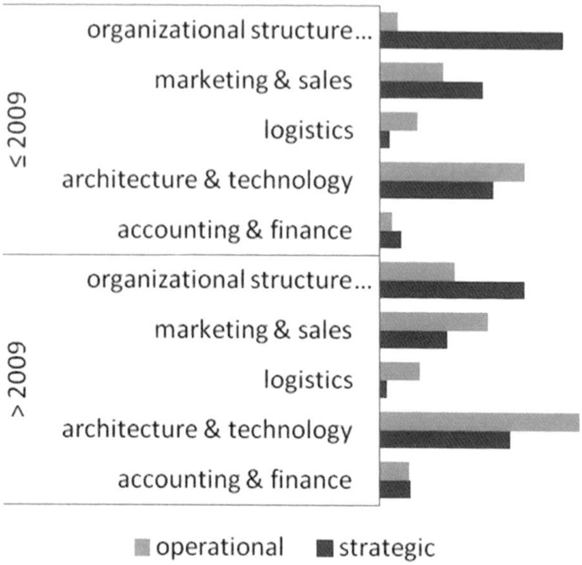

Fig. 5 Functional trend of investigated papers

clouds for papers on strategic BI. The terms *strategic*, *management*, *knowledge*, *competitive*, *planning*, *information*, and *decision* have a significant higher percentage in the papers on strategic BI. The most frequent strategic terms are *information*, *management*, and *decision*. They are interpretable as key elements stretching the relation of BI and strategic decisions. The terms *customer*, *marketing*, or *competitive* indicate a market orientation.

A wide and comprehensive scope is also evident for organizational concerns. There are aspects such as *maturity*, *learning*, *development*, or *predictive* representing a long-term and future-oriented emphasis. The adjectives *financial* and *economic* allow value and asset interpretations. An aggregated level of information is supported by high percentages of *planning*, *management*, and *knowledge*.

In contrast to the papers on strategic BI, the key issues shift to *process*, *technology*, and *information* in the papers on operational BI (cf. Fig. 7).

The papers on operational BI are notably distinct by *web*, *queries*, *process*, *realtime*, *traditional*, *optimization*, and *operational*. The relation of BI and operational decisions is strikingly characterized by the term *process*. It becomes apparent that processes define the source of information and narrow the scope of BI capabilities and operating activities. The importance of *tasks* and *execution* supports this pattern of argument. Thereby, *industrial*, *social* or *risk* indicate trends towards applications in an operational context. The association to technology aspects is strengthened due to operational ratios *web*, *queries*, *algorithm*, *platform*, *network*, and *internet*. The importance of *realtime* shows the demand for current and frequent information. A special distinguishing mark provides a consideration of effectiveness (accuracy and correctness of decisions) and efficiency (decision making cost). The percentage of *effective* is similar for both decision categories with a slight upward trend for the

Fig. 6 Word cloud on strategic BI

Fig. 7 Word cloud on operational BI

strategic perspective. The terms *efficiency* and *cost* have a higher importance in the operational context. Supporting arguments are time-related, because the time frame of decision making is more limited for operational decisions than in a strategic context. A decision's accuracy (*effective*) is necessary despite the short term background. This circumstance confirms, in combination with indices of an increasing complexity, the higher ratios of analysis terms (*analytics*, *evaluation*, or *olap*) for the papers on operational BI.

The discussion demonstrates that the relation of BI and strategic or operational decisions is characterized by the meaning of common terms and not by different terms. Papers on strategic and operational BI have, next to *data*, *business*,

Table 4 Common terms of investigated papers

Part of the BI definition	Common words
BI is a broad category applications, technologies, and processes for gathering, storing, accessing, and analyzing data...	Analytics, algorithm, architecture, concept, data, framework, implementation, integration, internet, mining, network, olap, platform, queries, report, software, system, technology, tools, warehousing, web
...to help business users make better decisions	Business, complex, customer, decision, development, effective, efficiency, evaluation, information, intelligence, knowledge, management, marketing, measurement, operational, performance, process, product, relationship, service, strategic, support

intelligence and *system,* 39 terms in common. This demonstrates an equal BI understanding for strategic and operational decision backgrounds. Table 4 illustrates this phenomenon by a common terms arrangement according to the definition of Hugh Watson [36] (cf. Sect. 2).

4.3 Discussion of Topics on Strategic and Operational BI

After the single-word analysis has shown content-related characteristics of the papers on strategic and operational BI, we subsequently analyze word groups to discuss topics on strategic and operational BI. Therefore, we modified the text mining transformation by building n-grams with a maximum of four terms. All n-grams with an occurrence greater or equal to ten were scanned for BI topics.

The most frequent word groups of the papers' abstracts on strategic and operational BI are *business intelligence*, *decision making*, *data mining*, and *data warehouse*. Such general BI terms are discarded, because the discussion focuses on representative topics.

Topics on strategic BI

The topics on strategic BI address different areas of organizational management and control. Figure 8 illustrates the determined strategic topics.

Strategic decision and *strategic management* [18] consider a management level perspective. *Information management* [20] references to executive functions of topics on strategic BI. There is also a relation to knowledge aspects like *knowledge management* [17] and *knowledge discovery* [1] as well as the use of knowledge to predict future trends or patterns (*predictive analytics* [13]).

The importance of competitiveness and information about actual market trends becomes apparent by *competitive intelligence* or *competitive advantage* [45]. *Business analytics* or *business models* [5] indicate the relevance of business information and analyses. The design and development of organizational aspects according to

Fig. 8 Topics on strategic BI

strategic considerations is pursued by *corporate performance management* [3] or *maturity models* [23].

The topics on strategic BI encompass concepts to coordinate internal applications (*enterprise resource planning*, *enterprise system*) [46] and the interaction to customers (*customer relationship management*, *customer data*) [21]. Technical concerns seem to be quality-oriented (*data quality* [42], *information quality* [31]) and secondary in the strategic context.

Topics on operational BI

The topics on operational BI focus in contrast to strategic BI on technological and application driven aspects (cf. Fig. 9).

The study objects of operational BI are *business processes* and *business operations*. These objects are investigated by two perspectives. *Operational business intelligence* [15] represents a BI view of analyzing data and information for decision purposes. *Business process management* [28] defines, implements, monitors, and optimizes business processes and operations. Hence, the combined consideration of BI and operational decisions leads to a merging of originally separated topics—business process management and business intelligence. The existence of *process mining* [35] supports this argumentation.

There are operational topics indicating a relevance of flexibility aspects. This concerns the capability of organizational change due to new market conditions (*organizational agility*) [6] and an architectural flexibility of software systems (*service oriented architecture*) [27].

Operational applications are characterized by *social media* [9], *sentiment analysis* [12], *risk management* [24], *shop floor* [16] and *situation awareness*

Fig. 9 Topics on operational BI

[4]. Social media and sentiment analysis address the customer interaction, risk management, and shop floor organizational activities. Situation awareness focuses on the business user.

From a data-oriented perspective, there is a relevance of *data management* [47] in operational context associated to *heterogeneous data sources*, *unstructured data* or *real time data*. The short-term time aspects are also expressed by *real time business intelligence* [37]. The topics of *big data* [5], *cloud computing* [2], *query processing*, and *workload management* [22] indicate a growing amount and complexity of data in an operational BI context.

5 Conclusion

Strategic and operational management tasks are characterized by different BI topics. The BI support of strategic decisions is associated with managerial concepts regarding corporate governance and information management. From a decision maker's perspective, strategic BI topics address the definition and adjustment of an organization's objectives. There are approaches to structure the goal accomplishment and to enhance the organizational capabilities in context of strategic management tasks.

Operational BI is not in such a mature state of the art. The topics suggest rather domains of activities than specify certain tasks of operational management to ensure a proper task execution or to employ tools or resources adequately. It remains unclear, whether and how operational BI can provide a task-oriented decision support effectively and efficiently. There is a coexistence of decision making, technology issues, process management, and domain specificity in an operational management context. This forces decision makers to consider manifold perspectives and to examine also e.g. business process-oriented experiences and knowledge. Given a high level of detail and differentiation of operational activities, the corresponding decision making exhibits a high complexity. Faced by the circumstances that BI publications investigate increasingly operational management activities, the research focus has to shift its attention to providing assistance to encounter that complexity and to jointly investigate different perspectives of operational decision making.

The motivation of contributions to operational BI is not only practice-oriented, but also of scientific interest. Decision makers are addressed by a systematic reference of BI topics according to information needs and managerial tasks. These findings are relevant for scientists to guide future research activities. Therefore, this chapter introduces a literature classification to discuss the status quo and development trends of BI towards an operational decision making. It is evident that there is a need of research in this context. Avenues of future BI research are the development and enhancement of organizational analysis and control concepts to support operational tasks. Common use cases concern core processes of manufacturing or service provision, support processes as well as project management activities. Further research on operational BI has to consider specific scenarios from a practical and generalizability from a scientific point of view.

References

1. Aggarwal N, Kumar A, Khatter H et al (2012) Analysis the effect of data mining techniques on database. Adv Eng Software 47(1):164–169
2. Baars H, Kemper H-G (2011) Ubiquitous computing—an application domain for business intelligence in the cloud? In: AMCIS 2011 proceedings, Detroit, MI, 4–8 Aug 2011
3. Brynjolfsson E, Hitt L, Kim HH (2011) Strength in numbers: How does data-driven decision-making affect firm performance? In: ICIS 2011 Proceedings, Shanghai, 4–7 Dec 2011
4. Castellanos M, Gupta C, Wang S et al (2012) A platform for situational awareness in operational BI. Decis Support Syst 52(4):869–883
5. Chen H, Chiang RHL, Storey VC (2012) Business intelligence and analytics: From big data to big impact. MISQ 36(4):1165–1188
6. Chen X, Siau K (2012) Effect of business intelligence and IT infrastructure flexibility on organizational agility. In: ICIS 2012 Proceedings, Orlando, FL, 16–19 Dec 2012
7. Cooper HM (1998) Synthesizing research: A guide for literature reviews. Sage, Thousand Oaks, CA
8. Davis JR, Imhoff C, White C (2009) Operational business intelligence: The state of the art. Beye NETWORK Research, Boulder, CO
9. Dinter B, Lorenz A (2012) Social business intelligence: a literature review and research agenda. In: ICIS 2012 Proceedings, Orlando, FL, 16–19 Dec 2012
10. Eckerson WW (2007) Best practices in operational BI: converging analytical and operational processes. TDWI Best Practices Report, Renton WA

11. Gorry GA, Scott-Morton MS (1971) A framework for management information systems. Sloan Manag Rev 13(1):55–72
12. Goul M, Marjanovic O, Baxley S et al (2012) Managing the enterprise business intelligence app store: sentiment analysis supported requirements engineering. In: 45th Hawaii international conference on system sciences, Maui, HI, 4–7 Jan 2012
13. Hair JF Jr (2007) Knowledge creation in marketing: the role of predictive analytics. Eur Bus Rev 19(4):303–315
14. Hayen RL (2008) Direction in business intelligence: an analysis of applications. In: AMCIS 2008 Proceedings, Toronto, 14–17 Aug 2008
15. Hänel T, Felden C (2012) Towards a stability of process oriented decision support concepts using the example of operational business intelligence. Paper presented at the Pre-ICIS BI congress 3: driving innovation through big data analytics, Orlando, FL, 16–19 Dec 2012
16. Hänel T, Felden C (2011) Limits or integration?—manufacturing execution systems and operational business intelligence. In: AMCIS 2011 proceedings, Detroit, MI, 4–8 Aug 2011
17. Hertlein M, Smolnik S, Von Kortzfleisch HFO (2011) Towards a framework for measuring knowledge management service productivity. In: ICIS 2011 proceedings, Shanghai, 4–7 Dec 2011
18. Isaev D (2010) Information support of corporate governance and strategic management using analytical software. IEEE Int Conf Intell Comput Intell Syst 3:44–48. doi:10.1109/ICICISYS.2010.5658550
19. Isik O, Jones MC, Sidorova A (2011) Business intelligence (BI) success and the role of BI capabilities. Intell Syst Account Finance Manag 18(4):161–176
20. Jourdan Z, Rainer RK, Marshall TE (2008) Business intelligence: an analysis of the literature. Inform Syst Manag 25:121–131
21. Saldanha T, Krishnan M (2011) BI and CRM for customer involvement in product and service development. In: ICIS 2011 proceedings, Shanghai, 4–7 Dec 2011
22. Krompass S, Kuno H, Dayal U et al (2007) Dynamic workload management for very large data warehouses: juggling feathers and bowling balls. In: Proceedings of the 33rd international conference on very large data bases, Vienna, 23–28 Sept 2007
23. Lahrmann G, Marx F, Winter R et al (2011) Business intelligence maturity: development and evaluation of a theoretical model. In: 44th Hawaii international conference on system sciences, Kauai, HI, 4–7 Jan 2011
24. Lee G, Kulkarni U (2011) Business intelligence in corporate risk management. In: AMCIS 2011 proceedings, Detroit, MI, 4–8 Aug 2011
25. Luhn HP (1958) A business intelligence system. IBM J Res Dev 2(4):314–319
26. Maghrabi RO, Oakley RL, Tambusamy R et al (2011) The role of business intelligence (BI) in service innovation: an ambidexterity perspective. In: AMCIS 2011 proceedings, Detroit, MI, 4–8 Aug 2011
27. Mahmoud T, Marx Gómez J, Rezgui A et al (2012) Enhanced BI systems with on-demand data based on semantic-enabled enterprise SOA. In: ECIS 2012 proceedings, Barcelona, 10–13 June 2012
28. Marjanovic O (2010) The importance of process thinking in business intelligence. Int J Bus Intell Res 1(4):29–46
29. Matei G (2010) A collaborative approach of business intelligence systems. J Appl Collab Syst 2(2):91–101
30. Mintzberg H (1973) The nature of managerial work. Harper & Row, New York
31. Mueller RM, Coppoolse D (2013) Using incentive systems to increase information quality in business intelligence: a quasi-experiment in the financial services industry. In: 46th Hawaii international conference on system sciences, Maui, HI, 7–10 Jan 2013
32. Seddon PB, Constantinidis D, Dod H (2012) How does business analytics contribute to business value? In: ICIS 2012 proceedings, Orlando, FL, 16–19 Dec 2012
33. Shollo A, Kautz K (2010) Towards an understanding of business intelligence. In: ACIS 2010 proceedings, Gardens Point, QLD, 1–3 Dec 2010

34. Simon HA (1960) The new science of management decision. Harper and Row, New York
35. van der Aalst W (2011) Using process mining to bridge the gap between BI and BPM. Computer 44(11):77–80
36. Watson HJ (2009) Tutorial business intelligence—past, present, and future. Commun Assoc Inform Syst 25(39):487–510
37. Watson HJ, Wixom BH, Hoffer J (2006) Real-time business intelligence: best practices at Continental Airlines. Inform Syst Manag 23(1):7–18
38. Watson HJ, Wixom BH (2007) The current state of business intelligence. Computer 40 (9):96–99
39. Webster J, Watson RT (2002) Analyzing the past to prepare for the future: writing a literature review. MISQ 26(2):xiii–xxiii
40. Wixom BH, Watson HJ (2010) The BI-based organization. Int J Bus Intell Res 1(1):13–28
41. White C (2006) The next generation of business intelligence: operational BI. BI Research, Ashland, OR
42. Yeoh W, Wang T-W, Verbitskiy Y (2012) Describing data quality problem through a metadata framework. In: AMCIS 2012 proceedings, Seattle, 9–11 Aug 2012
43. Yogev N, Fink L, Even A (2012) How business intelligence creates value. In: ECIS 2012 proceedings, Barcelona, 10–13 June 2012
44. Zhao Y (2012) R and data mining: examples and case studies. Elsevier, Amsterdam
45. Zhiqiang Z, Fader P, Padmanabhan B (2012) From business intelligence to competitive intelligence: inferring competitive measures using augmented site-centric data. Inform Syst Res 23(3):698–720
46. Zhou L (2012) Research on the integration application of business intelligence and ERP. In: International conference on management of e-commerce and e-government, Beijing, 20–21 Oct 2012
47. Zoder S (2011) Analytical master data management 2.0. In: AMCIS 2011 proceedings, Detroit, MI, 4–8 Aug 2011

On the Way from a Knowledge Discovery in Databases to a Predictive Analytics

Claudia Koschtial and Carsten Felden

Abstract Business Intelligence has "decision support" as a characterizing element. Decisions are done as a selection process based on alternatives. The choice depends on prospective developments whereby those developments are predicted with uncertainty. Due to this reason, forecasts are getting more into focus of the strategic and tactical level. But forecasts, usually based on Knowledge Discovery in Databases (KDD), are limited, yet. They often produce non-adequate results, which can lead to wrong decisions. Such a forecast quality demands further research in identifying improvements to increase reliability of forecast results and its usage in practice. This chapter modifies the Knowledge Discovery in Databases to improve the forecast quality. The associated process is supplemented by further steps to enhance the analyzed data set with additional future oriented data by using the KDD markup language. First results of an evaluation implementation at a German saving and loans bank shows motivating results.

Keywords Business Intelligence • Knowledge Discovery in Databases • Forecast • Data Mining • Predictive Analytics

1 Introduction

The daily work of managers is specified by the task of decision making. Decision makers act thereby in an area of conflict between organizational structures, budget restrictions, production changes, product innovations, changing customer needs, future oriented investment decisions, efficiency of production, selection of future oriented investments, etc. Management literature suggests that such a decision making can be supported by forecast techniques. But the financial crisis has shown that the complexity and dynamics of a crisis obstruct a reliable prognosis. Models are often multilayered and a little comprehensible, so that an appropriate usage is not possible. Also practical experiences show that the computed results do

C. Koschtial (✉) • C. Felden
Technische Universität Bergakademie Freiberg, Freiberg, Germany
e-mail: claudia.koschtial@bwl.tu-freiberg.de; carsten.felden@bwl.tu-freiberg.de

J.H. Mayer, R. Quick (eds.), *Business Intelligence for New-Generation Managers*,
DOI 10.1007/978-3-319-15696-5_2

not satisfy the decision makers due to the unsatisfactory prognosis quality. This leads to the situation that small and medium-size enterprises, but also large consolidated enterprises, avoid using prognosis models. Therefore, it is the goal of this chapter to improve the quality and thus the use of forecast models by an extension of Businesses Intelligence in sense of a Predictive Analytics process within enterprises.

Abilities and talents of decision makers, who determine the quality of decisions and problem solutions, can be embedded into a socio technical system. This frames the usage of information system by individuals or functions. Within this socio technical system it is the task of decision makers to specify goals, to evaluate alternatives, and to choose between possible alternatives. This is supported by Business Intelligence (BI) systems, which are described as abilities, technologies, applications, and procedures for supporting enterprise activities to assist the understanding of the business environment [5]. The more future oriented an analysis is, the more the concept of Knowledge Discovery in Databases (KDD) and in particular the Predictive Analytics, as a component of the Businesses Intelligence, are of importance and used in favor for decision support. Predictive Analytics is a kind of data analysis for strategic management. It is a process, which defines not only the collection of mass data, but also their processing by suitable statistical/analytical methods [6]. Its success depends on the available volume and quality of relevant historical and future oriented data and their modeling and concomitantly the reliability of the model in dynamic environments [20]. This research contributes to the discussion of forecast model quality to add value to the practice of information systems and to the scientific discussion about the quality improvement of forecast models and overall Businesses Intelligence.

The chapter is organized as follows: after a presentation of Business Intelligence based forecast process, application related obstacles are outlined (Sect. 2). Section 3 presents a modification of the KDD process in order to solve the addressed challenges. Section 4 uses the proposed concept in a case study. This case study describes Customer Relationship Management of a German saving and loans bank. The chapter ends with conclusions in Sect. 5.

2 Practical Implications of a Business Intelligence Based Forecast Process

This section discusses the forecast process support by Business Intelligence concepts and deals thereby with their obstacles. Based on these findings, the research objective is specified.

2.1 Forecasts within the Decision Process

A forecast task is to meet statements about the future. The necessity for a forecast is based on the uncertainty about future developments [2]. For this purpose, individual process steps are processed in order to gain a basis for decision making. The forecast process is just one element of an entire decision making process [18]. Simon identified the steps of decision making processes framed by rational behavior. A decision maker has to collect data about future conditions or consequences of defined events. Additionally, alternatives are to be determined, which consider appropriate probabilities. Distinctions to other existing models exist in the following aspects:

1. Decision makers look for available alternatives, since search costs have to be kept small. This leads to a prioritization and finally to non-optimal results.
2. It is not possible to occupy all alternatives with the probabilities of incidence and disbursements.
3. The value of a disbursement does not have to be a scalar parameter. It can be also a combination of individual values, which are defined as a vector.

The aspects mentioned by Simon led to the finding that decision making is restricted by limitations and not rational. He derived the following process steps, which are also seen as fundamental for the Business Intelligence concept [18]:

1. Provision of information (information acquisition and problem classification).
2. Design (determination of relevant criteria of the alternative selection).
3. Selection (determination of the most effective alternative).

These three phases were supplemented by the implementation phase of Simon himself and the monitoring phase by Book [10]. In addition, during the implementation of such a decision making process in Business Intelligence systems, the entwinement between users and information system has to be considered, too [1]. This includes for example, which information are offered to the user, for which purpose, or how to extent the model of the user.

2.2 Business Intelligence in the Forecast Process

Hans Peter Luhn defined the term Businesses Intelligence already in 1958 [14]. Intensive dissemination in theory and practice found this term however by a Gartner Group study in 1996 [1]. "Business Intelligence is providing decision makers with valuable information and knowledge by leveraging a variety of sources of data as well as structure and unstructured information [...] the term Business Intelligence has been in two different ways. It is sometimes used to refer to the product of the process or the information and knowledge that are useful to organizations for their business activities and decision making. On other occasions, BI is

Table 1 Information/methods of a business intelligence within the decision process

Decision phase	Information	Business intelligence
Information acquisition	Internal and external sources for planning and consolidation measures	Extraction/transformation/loading (ETL), Data Warehouse, KDD
Design	Knowledge and Experience for problem solving	Information analysis and modeling, intelligente agents
Selection	Business and implementation know how	
Implementation	Integration of potential users	Portals, analytical CRM
Monitoring	Understanding about socio technical systems	Reporting, online analytical processing (OLAP), visualization

used to refer to the process through which organizations obtains, analyzes, and distributes such information and knowledge" [17]. The definition shows the area of conflict between tools and individuals [13]. Following Table 1 clarifies the task supporting character of a Business Intelligence solution.

The determination, selection, and usage of relevant information and presented results depend on the respective user. In particular, during the forecast process, KDD has a high impact. KDD, as "nontrivial process of identifying valid, novel, potential useful, and ultimately understandable patterns in data" [9] is used for pattern recognition in order to be able to meet statements about the future.

2.3 Problem Statement

In particular practice oriented journals discuss regularly that the quality of the used forecast models is not sufficient. Prognoses are classified marginally better than dicing cubes [16]. It refers to the fact that forecasts are only suitable for a situation determination to date [15]. The DIW marked critically in 2009 that prognosis models provide only a small information value. Such discussions lead to the trend not to use these tools in decision making any longer [7]. In sense of designs science [11], we are proposing a modified KDD process in order to improve the forecast quality.

3 Conceptual Modification of the KDD Process to Improve the Forecast Quality

The usually used analytical model for supporting the forecast process is KDD, whose processing concept contains the processing and analysis of historical data. Goal of such a processing is finding samples and connections, which assist the forecast of future developments with a sufficient probability [8].

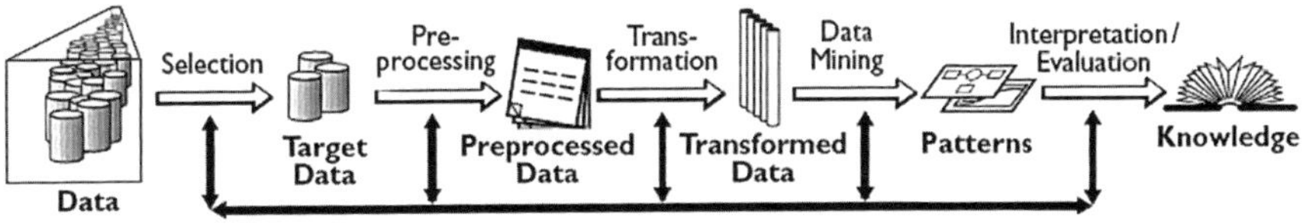

Fig. 1 KDD process model [9]

3.1 Knowledge Discovery in Databases Process Model

Independently of the procedural model discussed in the literature, individual comparable process steps can be identified within the KDD, which are shown in Fig. 1.

Data Mining, which is often used synonymously for KDD, is describing the pattern recognition in large data sets. It is usually arranged as automatic or semi-automatic process for solving problems like sales predictions [21]. It is noteworthy that the computer bound analytic methods used therein are becoming a matter of course. Thus, the current discussions turn away from explicit Data Mining procedures to more abstract terms like Predictive Analytics and due to this more into an application focus. Data Mining as such does not concentrate by definition on historical data (which is also not excluded). Earlier definitions state that Data Mining is a concept, which is able to anticipate future developments. But this is not reflected in its application; it is determined based on historical data, what happened historically. This history is applied to new data. Predictive Analytics extends this by future oriented descriptive elements explicitly, for example with data about demographic developments in context of customer analysis.

3.2 KDD Enhancements in Context of a Predictive Analytics

Analytics, also known as Business Analytics, describes the analysis and evaluation of data in context of a future oriented enterprise control [6]. The described approach of the common KDD as method of a data analysis and to the forecast implicates that there are no changes within manifested market processes and due to this in future markets. This assumption, typical for historically based approaches [12], has to be considered critically. Rather sudden shocks, as crisis charged features on the financial markets, or long term shifts of inquire relevant fundamental data (for example a demographic development), can endanger the forecast content of historical data. This development process can be e.g. clarified with age pyramids. They show substantial differences for Germany both in the intertemporal and in the interregional comparison. Essential accordingly straight for a regionally oriented enterprise is a region typical and long term anticipation of these structural changes, in order to be prepared for accompanying changes of the inventory and potential customers as well as their needs. Is generally valid: The past and due to this prognosticated values form the basis for strategic decision making, whereby data

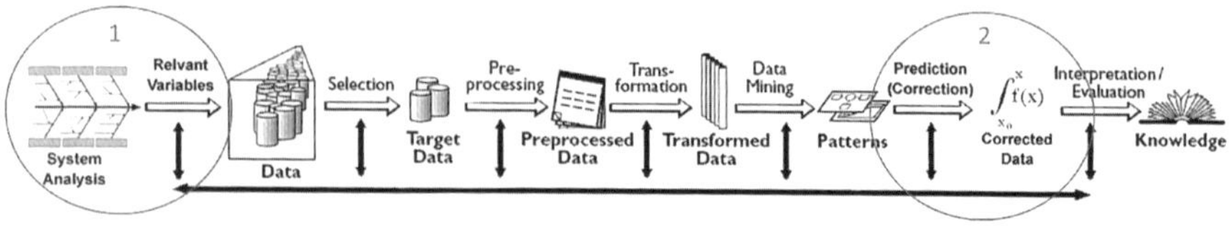

Fig. 2 Enhanced KDD process model in sense of predictive analytics

or analysis errors and/or wrong forecasts can lead to false decisions with strategic consequence. In order to reduce this risk, prognoses are to be supplemented by means of the KDD with information about intermediate as well as in the future foreseeable changes. This extension is the central thought of Predictive Analytics. An improvement in relation to the values of the classical KDD is obtained in particular by the extension and correction of the forecast model around future oriented data. In order to illustrate this correction calculation in context of an extended KDD processing concept, different possibilities exist.

Figure 2 shows that before the actual pattern analysis starts, it has to be analyzed whether the operational question, which can be answered by KDD, or if there are relevant changes of variables in relation to their initial value for the time of the emergence of the historical data (supplemental step system analysis (→ 1 in the figure)). As prerequisite step to the actual model building, all parts of a system have to be determined with their relations and their cooperation. This is a difference to the common Data Mining step. This means not just to identify unknown patterns in data, but rather the inclusion of possible well known patterns into the later forecast model (→ 2 in the figure). For this purpose, System Dynamics cause/effect diagrams [19] or Ishikawa diagrams [3] can be helpful. If there are no identified dependencies or relevant values of the subject matter period, the KDD process can proceed in its common steps. However, if changes in the period have to be considered, which can be prognosticated, a correction calculation must be done (supplemental step application of samples and correction), in order to achieve an as high prognosis quality as possible for the predicted data. To support this, the KDD Markup Language (KDDML) is used in order to realize the supplement of the model by appropriate meta data. Further probabilities can be put into the model to be able to describe certain events by more parameters, in order to describe future situations consciously.

4 Case Study: Customer Relationship Management in a German Saving and Loans

The case is based on anonymous customer data of a German savings and loans bank. The data are retrieved from their Data Warehouse and preprocessed as well as transformed according to the KDD process. During preprocessing incorrect data records are removed or data adjustments are implemented, if necessary. During the transformation, product instances are aggregated and converted from individuals to households or numerical values such as account balances are transformed into binary values, in order to receive the information about an account usage. On the basis of the transformed data, characteristic of current customers are identified, who already decided for an investment in the financial product Deka funds. Different Data Mining algorithms such as decision trees and artificial neural networks are applied.

A decision tree consists of a root, leaves, and branches. The root contains all data records; each data record contains all data which can be evaluated. Leaves are divided in accordance with the evaluation of an attribute with each individual data record [21]. Goal of this procedure is the selection of a dividing attribute to produce leaves with homogeneous data records [4]. The application of a decision tree shows that just 7 % of the overall private customers use the Deka funds, while the ratio among the customers, who possess also a savings agreement for building purposes, is already 22 %. Even if this sequence is included, sample statements can be derived toward an increased probability of sale from Deka funds at building savers. The temporal accumulation of the product conclusions is likewise examined. It is shown that all customers, who possessed both products, bought the savings agreement for building purposes first and thereafter the purchase of the Deka funds happened.

In contrast to it, an artificial neural network works as black box to a certain extent. Are procedure calculates a result, which can be used to forecast the purchase behavior of the Deka funds [4]. Both decision trees and artificial neural networks supply appropriate results, whereby the valuation criteria remain unsettled with the latter. Both can be used parallel and be chosen according to their forecast quality. The found samples can be applied to the customer data set in order to identify customers who do not possess Deka funds so far and, based on the historical data set, have a high relevant probability of to purchase such funds.

If it is identified for each product and each customer, whether and when he/she is a buyer (or not), the Customer Lifetime Value (CLV) of the customer can be calculated. Appropriate products are offered according to the specific interests and points in time to be able to manage the relationship to the customer during his/her lifetime (in the sense of the CLV). In relation to the principle of a uniform distribution this procedure offers the advantage that an improved allocation of resources can take place, because not all customers cause the same expenditure. The first trial of the described procedure is done without a purposeful and for the relationship of the savings bank valid basic correction of the forecast data. At this point, the principle of the Predictive Analytics sets.

The examined enhancement of common KDD to a Predictive Analytics can be compared on the basis of a CLV computation. With its accuracy, the necessity decreases of uncertainty conditioned adjustments and increases in response to the reliability of a CLV as decision basis for the Customer Relations Management. Depending upon demarcation of the forecast the received values can also affect the strategic business development. On this basis, a former campaign of the example

Table 2 Result comparison of the common and the modified KDD process

Customer ID	E	F	L	Prog_ Procukt_ A	Prog_ Dat_ A	Prog_ Procukt_ B	Prog_ Dat_ B	CLV	CLV-corrected
1399XXX	E	M	L	0		0		234.34	107.89
1428XXX	E	F	N	1	2012	0		5,043.34	5,043.34
1445XXX	E	M	N	1	2015	1	2011	10,003.23	8,763.99
1450XXX	E	F	W	0		0		−645.00	−623.45
1451XXX	G		N	0		0		0	0
1477XXX	E	F	L	1	2010	1	2012	1,534.20	1,534.20
1494XXX	E	M	N	0		1	2013	8,674.5	8,455.40
202576XXX	E	F	N	0		1	2010	375.44	375.44
1968711XXX	G		N	0		0		198.45	234.48
1517XXX	E	M	V	0		0		0	0
1525XXX	E	M	N	0		0		0	0
157XXX	E	M	N	1	2015	0		9,700.56	8,951.67

bank was done with the common and the modified KDD process to be able to compare the results.

Table 2 shows the CLV result of the common KDD process (column CLV) and the result of the modified KDD process (column CLV corrected). Including the majority of the test data, a correction of the CLV forecast took place. Since at several times customer data was extracted from the Data Warehouse, a comparison with actual results was possible based on the documented customer history. This comparison confirmed the more precise forecasts of the modified KDD process. Thus the descriptive modification of the KDD process makes a contribution for the increase of the efficiency of a value oriented banking business.

5 Conclusions

An implemented forecast model offers a systematic support, which is essential for successful enterprises. With the estimation of the necessary input data, Predictive Analytics offers the support and thus, decision support improvement potentials. This research project aims on a confrontation of the results of different forecast models and the comparison of their results.

This chapter contributes to the discussion of Business Intelligence supported forecast processes. The accuracy increase of the CLV, which is shown by comparing results of two approaches of prognosticating a CLV in the specified example, confirms the improvement potential by the modification of the KDD process. The processing concept is enhanced with two further steps: The first step contains the analysis of the source systems and their data. If this step shows the fact that a stable system is present, it will not be necessary to implement further adjustment.

Otherwise, corrective measures are necessary after the computation of the samples. The integration of additional data like demographic prognoses can be realized by the use of semantic approaches like KDDML.

Supplementing research is necessary regarding further application fields of the modified KDD process in the sense of a Predictive Analytics. Valid basic conditions and adjustments have to be tested in order to prove the usefulness and thus decision support potentials for applications. Besides, also basic conditions for the economically meaningful employment of the method have to be analyzed as the expenditure for the production of the prognosis rises.

References

1. Anandarajan M, Anandarajan A, Srinivasan CA (2004) Business intelligence techniques. A perspective from accounting and finance. Springer, Berlin
2. Armstrong JS (2001) Introduction. In: Armstrong JS (ed) Principles of forecasting: a handbook for researchers and practitioners. Springer, Berlin, pp 1–12
3. Bauer K (2005) KPI identification with fishbone enlightenment. DM Rev 15(3):12
4. Chakrabarti S, Witten IH, Cox E (2009) Data mining: know it all. Morgan Kaufmann, Burlington
5. Chamoni P, Gluchowski P (2006) Analytische Informationssysteme—Einordnung und Überblick. In: Chamoni P, Gluchowski P (eds) Analytische Informationssysteme: Business Intelligence-Technologien und -Anwendungen, 3rd edn. Springer, Berlin, pp 3–22
6. Davenport TH, Harris JG (2007) Competing on analytics—the new science of winning. Harvard Business School Press, Boston
7. Ebert F, Isnik Z (2010) Qualitative und quantitative Szenarioplanung als Grundlage der unternehmerischen Nachhaltigkeit. http://www.haufe.de/controllerwissen/controllermagazin/magazineItemDetail?editionID=1260365185.13&articleID=6. Accessed 31 July 2011
8. Fayyad U, Piatetsky-Shapiro G, Smyth P (1996) Knowledge discovery and data mining: towards a unifying framework. In: KDD proceedings, AAAI
9. Fayyad U, Piatetsky-Shapiro G, Smyth P (1996) The KDD process for extracting useful knowledge from volumes of data. Comm ACM 39(11):27–34
10. Hall DJ (2008) Decision makers and their need for support. In: Burstein F, Holsapple CW (eds) International handbooks on information systems. Springer, Berlin, pp 83–102
11. Hevner AR, March ST, Park J (2004) Design science in information systems research. MIS Q 28(1):75–105
12. Horsch A, Schulte M (2010) Wertorientierte Banksteuerung II: Risikomanagement, 4th edn. Frankfurt School, Frankfurt/M
13. Kemper H-G, Mehanna W, Unger C (2006) Business Intelligence—Grundlagen und praktische Anwendungen: Eine Einführung in die IT-basierte Managementunterstützung, 2nd edn. dpunkt, Wiesbaden
14. Luhn HP (1958) A business intelligence system. IBM J Oct(1958):314–319
15. Nissen N (2009) Fehlinvestition Konjunkturprognose? http://www.heise.de/tp/r4/artikel/30/30933/1.html. Accessed 7 July 2011
16. Plickert P, Bernau P (2010) Nur ein bisschen besser als Würfeln. http://www.faz.net/s/RubB8DFB31915A443D98590B0D538FC0BEC/Doc~E7ADDAB15913F436BAF82FB6620 16E18D~ATpl~Ecommon~Scontent.html. Accessed 7 July 2011
17. Sabherwal R, Becerra-Fernandez I (2010) Business intelligence. Wiley, Hoboken
18. Simon HA (1955) A behavioral model of rational choice. Q J Econ 69(1):99–118

19. Sterman JD (2000) Business dynamics: systems thinking and modeling for a complex world. McGraw Hill, Boston
20. Vogler-Ludwig K (2009) Prognosen ohne Zukunft. http://www.economix.org/PrognosenohneZukunft.pdf. Accessed 7 July 2011
21. Witten IH, Frank E (2005) Data mining. Elsevier, San Francisco

Design and Implementation of a Performance Measurement System for the German Trade Sector

Maurice Kügler and Christoph Nowakowski

Abstract Managers in today's trade companies need information management tools that provide them with relevant information in a flexible way. This chapter addresses this need by proposing a performance measurement system particularly suited to managers' information needs in the German trade sector. Their information needs are determined by applying the success factor method and by analyzing empirical success factor research on the German trade sector. According to the identified information needs, the trade scorecard (TSC) is proposed, a performance measurement system for managers in the German trade sector. The TSC is then implemented as a prototype in a business intelligence environment that supports flexible, real-time access to company data.

Keywords German trade sector • Performance management • Performance measurement management

1 Introduction

The German trade sector is known for its intense competition. While revenues stay rather static, sales floors are being expanded at the same time, leading to a decline in productivity per area unit. This is a reason for the predatory competition experienced in the German trade sector in the last decade [10]. One result of this fierce competition is market consolidation in the trade sector, leading to a rise in mergers and acquisitions, to a more dynamic market environment, and finally to a lower number of trade companies with increasing size [27]. In addition, trade companies are intensifying their links to partners up and down their supply chains in order to gain a competitive advantage [13]. Consequently, trade companies' relationships to

M. Kügler (✉)
EBS Business School, Wiesbaden, Germany

Boston College, Chestnut Hill, MA, USA
e-mail: maurice.kuegler@ebs.edu

C. Nowakowski
BearingPoint, Frankfurt, Germany
e-mail: christoph.nowakowski@bearingpoint.com

J.H. Mayer, R. Quick (eds.), *Business Intelligence for New-Generation Managers*,
DOI 10.1007/978-3-319-15696-5_3

their suppliers as well as customers gain in importance. The aforementioned developments in the German trade sector lead to changing demands for trade companies' management and their supporting entities. A high degree of flexibility in decision making is needed when it comes to steering trade companies today. Key to success in decision making flexibility is providing management with information in a timely manner [1]. Hence, managers in today's trade companies are in need of information that provide them with relevant information in a flexible way.

This chapter addresses this need by proposing a performance measurement system (PMS) suited to managers' information needs in the German trade sector and implementing this performance measurement system in a business intelligence (BI) environment that supports flexible, real-time access to company data. In order to achieve this, managers' information needs are first being determined by identifying the success factors of the German trade sector. Based on this, a trade-sector specific PMS, the trade scorecard, is being proposed. The trade scorecard is then implemented as a prototype. The remainder of this chapter is structured as follows: In the next section, the theoretical background on information needs, business intelligence, and performance measurement systems is given. The subsequent section presents the design of the trade scorecard. In the following section, the prototypal implementation is described, before the last section concludes this chapter.

2 Theoretical Background

The following sections provide some background on managers information needs, performance measurement systems, and business intelligence.

2.1 Determining Managers' Information Needs

In order to enable executives in the trade sector to successfully steer their organizations through the highly dynamic market environment, understanding their information needs is of vital importance [30]. On the one hand, in today's data-driven business environment there is a tendency towards decision makers' information overflow, and on the other hand, business executives still complain about a lack of relevant information [17]. Hence, determining executives' actual information needs is a necessary first step in developing a performance measurement system. One method for assessing people's information needs is the method of critical success factors (CSFs). This method goes back to Daniel [6] who states that an organization's success is dependent on a limited set of strategic factors. Due to the importance of these factors, executives' information needs can be derived from them. Rockart [38] further advances Daniel's approach and defines as follows: "Critical success factors thus are, for any business, the limited number of areas in which results, if they are satisfactory, will ensure successful competitive performance for the organization. They are the few key areas where 'things must go right' for the business to flourish. If results in these areas are not adequate, the organization's efforts for the period will be less than desired" ([38], p. 85). Thus, CSFs identify areas that should receive executives' attention and should be continually measured. CSFs, however, are not necessarily confined to one organization. Leidecker and Bruno's [26] research suggests to differentiate between (1) CSFs that are valid for one organization, (2) CSFs that are valid for a whole sector, and (3) CSFs that are valid across sectors. Since this chapter aims to develop a PMS that is valid for one sector (i.e. the German trade sector), the remainder of this chapter focuses on sector-specific CSFs.

2.2 *Performance Measurement Systems*

Against the background of the changing demands for managers of German trade companies and the technological advances of the recent decades, organizational information provision is at risk of providing managers with a vast amount of data that they cannot make efficient use of—such a situation is referred to as information overload [7]. This challenge has been frequently reported to be one of the main deficiencies in the management support functions of the German trade sector (e.g., [19, 34]). One of the main tools for aggregating and compiling information in an adequate, compact way to inform managers are PMSs. A PMS can be defined as a meaningful set of performance indicators that provide information on different dimensions of an organizational process or area of interest [36]. PMSs in the trade sector have in recent years been criticized for their lack of relevant measures. They have a tendency to report on a high number of irrelevant measures, leading to managers not using the available PMSs as an information source for decision-making [41]. Morschett [31] and Liebmann et al. [27] further criticize the lack of qualitative, non-financial performance indicators in current PMSs for the trade sector. The PMS developed in this chapter aims at addressing the aforementioned deficiencies.

2.3 *Business Intelligence*

Given the vast amount of data that resides within organizations and their information systems today, analytical applications help corporate planners to extract insightful information from their data sources [47]. While management support systems have been the subject of information systems (IS) research since the 1960s, the last decade has witnessed the evolution of corporate-wide BI infrastructures that form the basis of powerful analytical applications. BI—a term coined by the Gartner Group in 1989 [50]—is used as an umbrella term to describe concepts and methods for improving business decision making by using fact-based support [33, 37]. Several BI frameworks have been developed to systematically capture the BI concept and its main constituents. Devlin [8] and Kimball et al. [24] identified the technical BI components, which mainly comprise of the data warehouse and the technical processing of structured data. Watson and Wixom [50] distinguish two primary activities to illustrate BI: "getting data in" and "getting data out". While "getting data in" describes the transformation of data from heterogeneous sources into an integrated data warehouse, "getting data out" refers to business users and applications accessing data with the objective to perform enterprise reporting, to conduct customized queries or to engage in predictive modelling [50]. In line with Negash [32], BI can be defined as "systems [that] combine data gathering, data storage, and knowledge management with analytical tools to present complex internal and competitive information to planners and decision makers" (p. 178). BI is designed to assist individual users in processing vast quantities of data when making decisions in an organizational context [51]; consequently, BI enables improved organizational action and decision making [5]. Relating BI to PMSs, one can say that PMSs determine the content that is technically being represented by BI tools.

3 Design of a Performance Measurement System for the German Trade Sector

This section conceptualizes a balanced scorecard-based PMS particularly suited for the German trade sector, called the trade scorecard (TSC). First, the design approach that was followed for developing the TSC will be introduced, before the TSC itself will be presented.

3.1 Design Approach for Trade Scorecard

The TSC is based on the widely accepted balanced scorecard (BSC) approach [21–23] and the success factor based balanced scorecard (SFBSC) proposed by Hornung, Mayer, and Wurl [15, 16, 29, 53, 54]. The TSC consists of one financial and several non-financial perspectives. It is developed in three phases (Fig. 1):

1. First, the trade sector-specific success factors are assessed in order to determine the non-financial perspectives of the TSC. The success factor method [38] allows the TSC to explicitly consider German trade sector-specific managerial information needs.
2. Second, the success factors are being operationalized by means of key performance indicators (KPIs). Two major requirements for selection and arrangement of the KPIs during this phase were offering a high level of transparency and

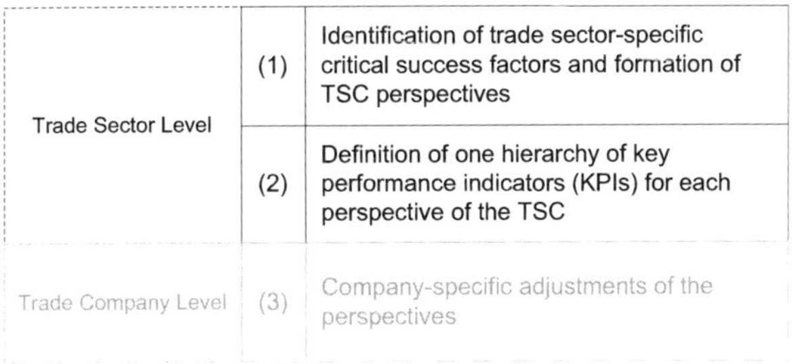

Fig. 1 Three phases of trade scorecard (TSC) development

clarity while still providing managers with fine-grained information enabling them to derive concrete measures [31]. The TSC brings these requirements in line by proposing one KPI hierarchy per perspective. KPI hierarchies provide managers with a quick overview on certain organizational areas of interest while also allowing them to dig deeper into specific fields of interest by drilling down certain KPIs, if needed. This approach assures that the resulting PMS offers comprehensive information and is compact at the same time.

3. Third, the TSC needs to be adjusted to the specificities of a particular company. Hereby, the KPI hierarchies developed in phase 2 are being adapted in close cooperation with the company's top management. This phase is necessary in order to assure that the TSC addresses a target company's specific information needs. This third phase of the TSC's design approach addresses the particularities of a specific company. This chapter's goal, however, is the development of a PMS with sector-wide applicability. Hence, the third phase of the TSC's design approach is not being given any further attention in the remainder of this chapter.

3.2 *Sector-Specific Success Factors of the German Trade Sector and the Formation of the TSC Perspectives*

Since its beginnings in the 1960s [6], success factor research has received great research attention in Germany [42]. Success factor research focusing on the German trade sector started to emerge in the 1970s [40]. Moreover, success factor research became a major research stream in German trade research [48]. Besides a number of studies that investigated CSFs of particular trade companies (e.g., [3, 9, 35, 49]), the studies by Wölk [52], Kalka [20], and Hurth [18] determined CSFs of the German trade sector by empirically assessing a number of trade companies. Additionally, Kube [25] conducted a meta-analysis of empirical success factor research on the German trade sector. Since Kalka's [20] results are limited to CSFs in Marketing, her results are too specific for our research purposes and are therefore not further considered in the following. Consequently, the sector-specific success factors of the German trade sector are based on the results of Hurth [18], Kube [25], and Wölk [52].

In the following, the CSFs that are part of the TSC are briefly introduced:

1. *Market Potential*: This CSF considers the demand structure in the catchment area of a trade business. Factors like density of population, income level, or buying power play important roles in this context.
2. *Competitive Environment*: This CSF reflects the intensity of a trade business' competition in its local environment.
3. *Location Quality*: This CSF covers all aspects surrounding the physical location of a trade business, such as transport connection, accessibility, or availability of parking spaces.
4. *Branch Size*: The branch size refers to the size of the floorspace of a trade business. Economies of scale play an important role with regard to this CSF.
5. *Service Level*: This CSF is concerned with the services that a trade business offers to their customers, in addition to offering purchasable products. This CSF is critical for customer interaction and customer satisfaction.
6. *Assortment*: The assortment is said to be the most important CSF for a trade business. Two important aspects to consider regarding a trade business' assortment are the product mix width and the product mix breadth.
7. *Pricing Policy*: This CSF considers the pricing strategy that a trade business pursues. Pricing image and margins are two of the factors that need to be taken into account with regard to pricing.
8. *Personnel Policy*: The personnel policy CSF comprises all issues regarding a trade business' human capital, such as personnel intensity, demographic personnel structure, personnel quality, or personnel productivity.

The eight identified CSFs of the German trade sector point out those areas that trade companies' top managers should pay particular attention to. Hence, these areas represent the trade sector-specific information needs that should be considered in a PMS that focuses on the German trade sector.

In order to keep the TSC's non-financial perspectives to a manageable number, the eight CSFs are further aggregated into a number of non-financial perspectives in a next step. Hereby, one or more CSFs are being transferred into one perspective of the TSC based on their content fit. The CSFs that are transferred into one perspective in this step are further detailed during operationalization of the perspectives into KPI hierarchies (phase 2 in Fig. 1). The results of the aggregation step (phase 1 in Fig. 1) are visualized in Fig. 2.

The following section will provide an overview of the TSC's financial perspective. The subsequent section will introduce the employee perspective to illustrate how the KPI hierarchies of the TSC's non-financial perspectives are composed. Due to space limitations, only one non-financial perspective will be shown in more detail in this chapter.

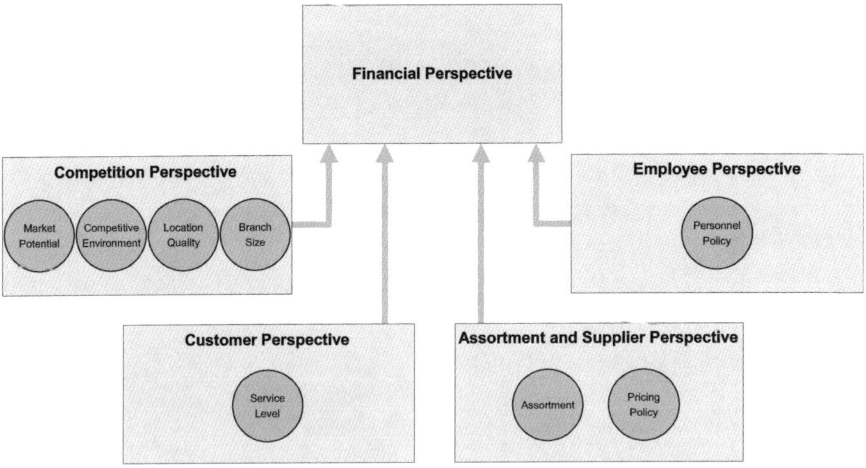

Fig. 2 The TSC perspectives

3.3 The Financial Perspective

Different financial KPIs, such as net profit ratio or return on equity, could be used as the main performance indicator of the TSC's financial perspective. Zentes et al. [55] support this notion when stating as follows: "There is no difference in principle, in measuring the financial performance of the retail industry and other industries: liquidity ratios, return ratios, earnings coverage ratios, value metrics" (p. 317). The TSC utilizes the Economic Value Added (EVA) [45], which can be defined as the "residual income left over from operating profits after the cost of capital has been subtracted" ([44], p. 49). The EVA is used by major German trade companies as their main financial performance indicator (e.g., [10]). It can mathematically be disaggregated into a KPI hierarchy by breaking down the EVA formula into its constituents. The EVA is being calculated as the net operating profit after taxes (NOPAT) minus capital costs. The capital costs can in turn be calculated by multiplying the invested capital (IC) with the weighted average cost of capital (WACC) [4, 43, 45, 46]. The resulting first two layers of the TSC's financial perspective is presented in Fig. 3. The KPI hierarchy is further disaggregated in the full version of the TSC. However, this chapter will not go into further details on the TSC's financial perspective due to space limitations.

3.4 The Non-financial Perspectives: Key Performance Indicator Hierarchies Exemplified

In order to enable the aggregation of all KPIs of one perspective into one main KPI, a mechanism is needed that allows to consolidate the results of several KPIs no

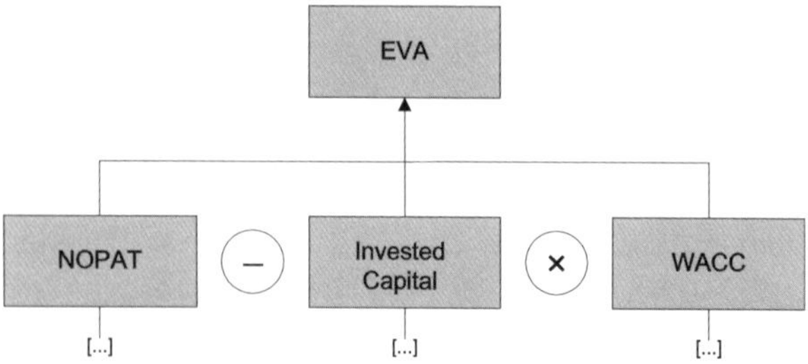

Fig. 3 The financial perspective of the TSC (excerpt of the first two layers)

Table 1 Example of a KPI data sheet

ID	Definition	Description	Target value	Actual value	Weighting factor	Grade of target achievement (GTA)
...	...	...	...	...	...	...

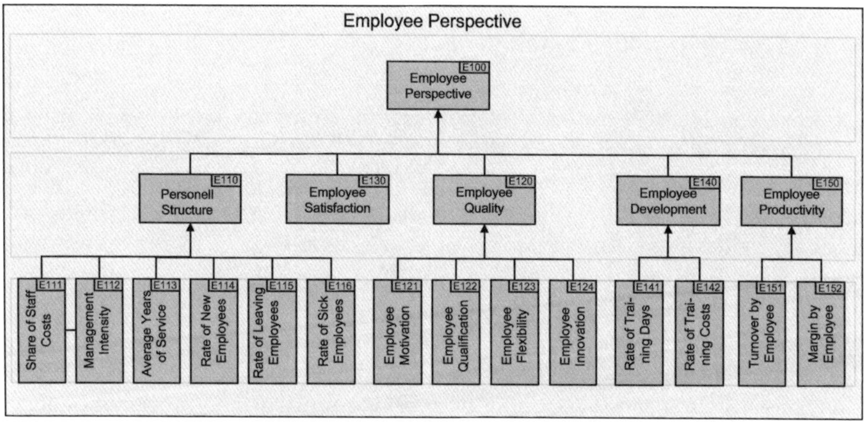

Fig. 4 The employee perspective as an example of a non-financial perspective

matter what kind of measurement it is measured with. To ensure this, the TSC approach utilizes grades of target achievement (GTAs) and weighting factors. The GTAs are determined by comparing actual versus target values for each single KPI included in a KPI hierarchy. Besides the target value, the actual value, and the resulting GTA, the TSC approach suggests to define each KPI by means of a formula as well as a detailed description. The resulting KPI data sheet that should be compiled for each of the non-financial perspectives of the TSC is exemplified in Table 1.

Following the logic of GTAs and weighting factors, each KPI that consists of several KPIs is calculated by multiplying each KPI's GTA with its weighting factor. The weighting factors of all the KPIs that form a higher-level KPI must add up to 100 %. As an example, the KPI *employee productivity* (E150 in Fig. 4) is composed of the KPIs *turnover by employee* (E151 in Fig. 4) and *margin by employee* (E152 in

Fig. 4). Assuming weighting factors of 50 % for both KPIs and GTAs of 80 % for E151 and 90 % for E152, the GTA for E150 would be as follows: $(0.5 \times 0.8) + (0.5 \times 0.9) = 85\ \%$.

The KPIs for the non-financial perspectives of the TSC are proposed based on an analysis of the German trade research literature. The full version of the TSC includes completed data sheets for each non-financial perspective, covering a total of 120 KPIs including their definitions and detailed descriptions. As an example, Fig. 4 depicts the KPI hierarchy of the TSC's employee perspective.

4 Prototypal Implementation in a Business Intelligence Environment

In order to demonstrate the PMS's technical feasibility, the TSC is implemented in a business intelligence environment as a prototype. The leading providers of business intelligence software are IBM, Microsoft, MicroStrategy, Oracle, SAP, SAS, and Teradata [12, 39]. The two main building blocks of a business intelligence environment are (1) data management, typically represented by a data warehouse, and (2) information access. Current data management solutions include IBM Data Warehouse, Microsoft SQL Server, Oracle Database, the SAP NetWeaver Business Warehouse (SAP BW), SAP HANA and Teradata [2]. Information access can be provided by IBM Cognos BI, Microsoft BI, MicroStrategy BI, Oracle BI Server, SAP BusinessObjects BI, and SAS Analytics [39].

Although the prototypal implementation of the TSC could certainly have been implemented in any of the aforementioned business intelligence environments, we decided to base the prototypal implementation on the SAP NetWeaver 7.0 Information Integration environment [28], combined with its BusinessObjects extensions [14]. In order to make managers' use of and interaction with the PMS as easy and convenient as possible, the PMS is being implemented as a management dashboard. A dashboard can be defined as "a visual display of the most important information needed to achieve one or more objectives" ([11], p. 34). The prototypal implementation's main components are the following (Fig. 5):

- *Data Management*: Data is stored in an SAP BW. Data from different data sources can be transferred into the SAP BW through a diverse set of interfaces.
- *Information Access*: The information access layer consists of the SAP BusinessObjects applications Xcelsius, Live Office, Web Intelligence, and Universe Designer, which are part of the SAP BusinessObjects Enterprise Platform. Data in these tools is being transferred through the Central Management Server (CMS), a central component of the SAP BusinessObjects Enterprise Platform that, among others, offers user management functionalities. The Universe Designer provides the SAP BusinessObjects Enterprise Platform with data access to the data stored in the SAP BW. Using this data, Web Intelligence allows users to build, edit, and manage real-time reports. Hence, these reports

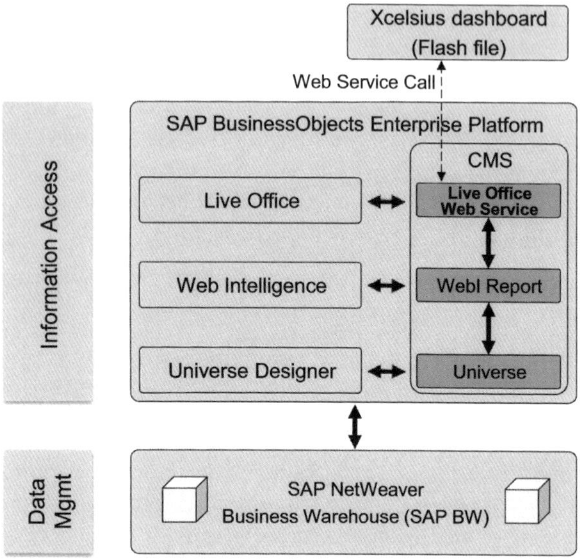

Fig. 5 BI architecture for prototypal implementation in SAP BusinessObjects

display the most current report results based on the data stored in the underlying SAP BW. The front-end tool Live Office is a plug-in for Microsoft Excel allowing to create Xcelsius dashboards in a rather user-friendly way. The created Xcelsius dashboards can then be exported into several different file formats (e.g., Flash file). Figure 5 gives an overview on the BI architecture used for the prototypal implementation of the TSC in SAP BusinessObjects.

An Xcelsius dashboard file, for example in Flash format, which was created following the above described procedure, can be displayed by any web browser that supports Flash files. Given that the uniform resource locator (URL) of the CMS was set correctly in the Flash file, the Xcelsius dashboard will, when opened, display its KPIs based on the backend data that it requests from the SAP BW in real-time. The prototypal dashboard implementation is limited to the financial perspective of the TSC. It thereby implements a KPI hierarchy based on the three main components of the EVA formula, namely NOPAT, IC and WACC. Figure 6 shows a screenshot of the Xcelsius dashboard representing the financial perspective of the TSC. The non-financial perspectives could be implemented in a similar manner.

5 Conclusion and Outlook

Managers in today's trade companies are in need of information management tools that provide them with relevant information in a flexible way. This chapter addresses this need by proposing a PMS particularly suited to managers' information needs in the German trade sector. Their information needs were determined by

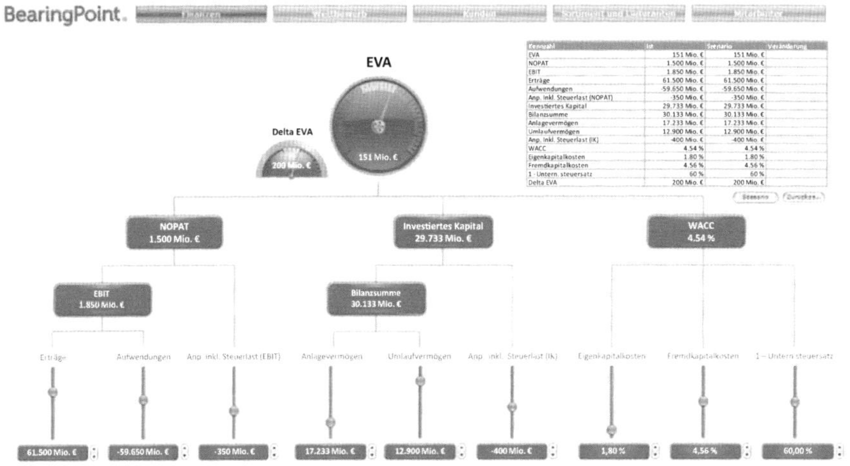

Fig. 6 Screenshot Xcelsius dashboard

applying Rockart [38] success factor method and analyzing the empirical success factor research on the German trade sector. According to the identified information needs, the trade scorecard was proposed, a PMS particularly suited to managers in the German trade sector. The TSC was then implemented as a prototype in a business intelligence environment that supports flexible, real-time access to company data. A next step in this research endeavor could involve the implementation of the TSC's non-financial perspectives. Furthermore, managers using the TSC in their daily routines could be interviewed in order to assess the extent of their use as well as the performance improvements that are observable in terms of, for example, managers' decision quality.

Acknowledgments The authors would like to thank the Business Intelligence team of BearingPoint GmbH (http://www.bearingpoint.com/de-de/) for supporting this research.

References

1. Ahlert D, Kenning P (2007) Handelsmarketing—Grundlagen der marktorientierten Führung von Handelsbetrieben. Springer, Berlin
2. Beyer MA, Edjlali R (2014) Magic quadrant for data warehouse database management systems. Gartner RAS core research notes. Gartner, Stamford, CT
3. Bolten J, Kennerknecht R, Spiller A (2006) Perspectives of small retailers in the organic market: customer satisfaction and customer enthusiasm. Paper presented at the 98th EAAE seminar—marketing dynamics within the global trading system: new perspectives, Chania, Crete, Greece
4. Brealey RA, Myers SC, Allen F (2008) Principles of corporate finance, 9th edn. McGraw-Hill, Boston, MA

5. Burton B, Geishecker L, Schlegel K, Hostmann B, Austin T, Herschel G, Soejarto A, Rayner N (2006) Business intelligence focus shifts from tactical to strategic. Gartner, Stamford, CT
6. Daniel DR (1961) Management information crisis. Harv Bus Rev 39(5):111–121
7. Dean D, Webb C (2011) Recovering from information overload. McKinsey Q 2011:80–88
8. Devlin B (1997) Data warehouse: from architecture to implementation. Addison-Wesley, Reading, MA
9. Eickhoff M, Eickhoff M (1997) Erfolgsforschung im Bekleidungseinzelhandel: Eine empirische Analyse erfolgreicher Unternehmen im deutschen und US-amerikanischen Facheinzelhandel mit Oberbekleidung, vol 23, Schriften zu Distribution und Handel. P. Lang, Frankfurt am Main
10. Elfers J (2007) Bewertung von Handelsunternehmen. In: Drukarczyk J, Ernst D (eds) Branchenorientierte Unternehmensbewertung. Vahlen, München, pp 75–132
11. Few S (2006) Information dashboard design: the effective visual communication of data. O'Reilly, Cambridge
12. Gartner (2014) Gartner says worldwide business intelligence and analytics software market grew 8 percent in 2013. http://www.gartner.com/newsroom/id/2723717. Accessed 12 June 2014
13. Hertel J, Zentes J, Schramm-Klein H (2005) Supply-Chain-Management und Warenwirtschaftssysteme im Handel. Springer, Berlin
14. Hilgefort I (2009) Integrating SAP BusinessObjects XI 3.1 tools with SAP NetWeaver. Galileo, Bonn
15. Hornung K, Mayer JH (1999) Erfolgsfaktoren-basierte Balanced Scorecards zur Unterstützung einer wertorientierten Unternehmensführung. Controlling 11(8–9):389–398
16. Hornung K, Mayer J (2000) Wertorientierte Führungsinformationssysteme auf Basis Erfolgsfaktoren-basierter Balanced Scorecards. Controller News o. Jg. (1):2–6
17. Horváth P (2009) Controlling. Vahlens Handbücher der Wirtschafts- und Sozialwissenschaften, 11th edn. Vahlen, München
18. Hurth J (1998) Erfolgsfaktoren im mittelständischen Einzelhandel. Dt. Fachverl, Frankfurt am Main
19. Hurth J (2006) Controlling im Handel. In: Zentes J (ed) Handbuch Handel: Strategien—Perspektiven—internationaler Wettbewerb. Gabler, Wiesbaden, pp 873–893
20. Kalka R (1996) Marketingerfolgsfaktoren im Facheinzelhandel. Dt. Univ., Wiesbaden
21. Kaplan RS, Norton DP (1992) The balanced scorecard—measures that drive performance. Harv Bus Rev 70(1):71–79
22. Kaplan RS, Norton DP (1993) Putting the balanced scorecard to work. Harv Bus Rev 71(5):134–147
23. Kaplan RS, Norton DP (1996) The balanced scorecard: translating strategy into action. Harvard Business School Press, Boston, MA
24. Kimball R, Ross M (2002) The data warehousing toolkit. Wiley, New York
25. Kube C (1991) Erfolgsfaktoren in Filialsystemen: Diagnose und Umsetzung im strategischen Controlling. Gabler, Wiesbaden
26. Leidecker JK, Bruno AV (1984) Identifying and using critical success factors. Long Range Plann 17(1):23–32
27. Liebmann H-P, Zentes J, Swoboda B (2008) Handelsmanagement, 2nd edn. Vahlen, München
28. Marx Gómez JC, Rautenstrauch C, Cissek P (2009) Einführung in business intelligence mit SAP-NetWeaver 7.0. Springer, Berlin
29. Mayer JH (1999) Führungsinformationssysteme für die internationale Management-Holding. Gabler Edition Wissenschaft. Deutscher Universitäts, Wiesbaden
30. Mayer JH, Bischoff S, Winter R, Weitzel T (2012) Extending traditional EIS use to support mobile executives online and offline. MIS Q Exec 11(2):87–96
31. Morschett D (2004) Retail-performance-measurement—Konzepte und Perspektiven des Prozess-Controllings im Handel. In: Zentes J, Biesiada H, Schramm-Klein H (eds)

Performance leadership im Handel, vol 19, Zukunft im Handel. Dt. Fachverl, Frankfurt am Main, pp 63–92
32. Negash S (2004) Business intelligence. Comm Assoc Inform Syst 13:177–195
33. Negash S, Gray P (2008) Business intelligence. In: Burstein FH, Clyde W (eds) Handbook on decision support systems 2. Springer, Berlin, pp 175–193
34. Neidhart M, Morschett D, Biesiada H (2006) Retail-performance-measurement—Neuere Controllingkonzepte zur Messung der Performance in Handelsunternehmen. In: Zentes J (ed) Handbuch Handel: Strategien—Perspektiven—internationaler Wettbewerb. Gabler, Wiesbaden, pp 895–918
35. Olbrich R (1994) Erfolgspositionen im Lebensmittelhandel—Ergebnisse und Konsequenzen einer repräsentativen Befragung. Die Betriebswirtschaft (DBW) 54(4):425–442
36. Perkmann M, Neely A, Walsh K (2011) How should firms evaluate success in university–industry alliances? A performance measurement system. R&D Manag 41(2):202–216
37. Raisinghani MS (2004) Business intelligence in the digital economy: opportunities, limitations and risks. IGI, Hershey, PA
38. Rockart JF (1979) Chief executives define their own data needs. Harv Bus Rev 57(2):81–93
39. Sallam RL, Tapadinhas J, Parenteau J, Yuen D, Hostmann B (2014) Magic quadrant for business intelligence and analytics platforms. Gartner RAS core research notes. Gartner, Stamford, CT
40. Schröder H (1994) Erfolgsfaktorenforschung im Handel. Stand der Forschung und kritische Würdigung der Ergebnisse. Marketing—Zeitschrift für Forschung und Praxis (ZFP) 16(2): 89–106
41. Schröder H (2006) Handelscontrolling in Theorie und Praxis. In: Reinecke S (ed) Handbuch Marketingcontrolling—Effektivität und Effizienz einer marktorientierten Unternehmensführung. Gabler, Wiesbaden
42. Steinle C, Schmidt C, Lawa D (1995) Erfolgsfaktorenkonzepte und ihre Relevanz für Planungssysteme. Das Wirtschaftsstudium (WISU) 24(4):311–323
43. Stern JM, Stewart GB, Chew DH (1995) The EVA financial management system. J Appl Corp Finance 8(2):32–46
44. Stern Stewart & Co. (1994) Stern Stewart EVA round table. J Appl Corp Finance 7(2):46–70
45. Stewart GB (1991) The quest for value: the EVA management guide. Harper Business, New York
46. Stewart GB (1994) EVA: fact and fantasy. J Appl Corp Finance 7(2):71–84
47. Trkman P, McCormack K, Oliveira MPV, Ladeira MB (2010) The impact of business analytics on supply chain performance. Decis Support Syst 49(3):318–327
48. Trommsdorff V, Herm S (2006) 20 Jahre Suche nach Erfolgsfaktoren im Handel. In: Trommsdorff V (ed) Handelsforschung 2006, pp 15–23
49. Wahle P (1991) Erfolgsdeterminanten im Einzelhandel: Eine theoriegestützte, empirische Analyse strategischer Erfolgsdeterminanten, unter besonderer Berücksichtung des Radio- und Fernsehfacheinzelhandels, vol 12, Marktorientierte Unternehmensführung. P. Lang, Frankfurt am Main
50. Watson HJ, Wixom BH (2007) The current state of business intelligence. IEEE Comput 40(9):96–99
51. Watson HJ, Fuller C, Ariyachandra T (2004) Data warehouse governance: best practices at Blue Cross and Blue Shield of North Carolina. Decis Support Syst 38(3):435–450
52. Wölk A (1992) Erfolgsfaktoren kleiner und mittlerer Unternehmen im Einzelhandel—Eine empirische Studie. In: Trommsdorff V (ed) Handelsforschung 1992. Gabler, Wiesbaden
53. Wurl H-J, Mayer JH, Müller G (2001) Branchenspezifische Erfolgsfaktoren-basierte Balanced Scorecards. KPMG Consulting, Frankfurt a. M
54. Wurl H, Mayer J (2000) Gestaltungskonzept für Erfolgsfaktoren-basierte Balanced Scorecards. Zeitschrift für Planung (ZP) 11(1):1–22
55. Zentes J, Morschett D, Schramm-Klein H (2007) Strategic retail management: text and international cases. Gabler, Wiesbaden

Applicability of Environmental Scanning Systems: A Systematic List Approach to Requirements Criteria

Stefan Bischoff, Jörg H. Mayer, Timm Weitzel, and Reiner Quick

Abstract The increasing volatility of their companies' environment is a growing concern for executives. Environmental scanning systems should enable them to focus earlier on emerging threats and opportunities. A lack of applicability means that concepts often go unused in practice. But what does applicability mean for environmental scanning systems design? Adhering to the design science paradigm, this article contributes to better information systems (IS) design by developing a systematic list approach to requirements criteria that specify the applicability of environmental scanning systems. The criteria are derived from the principle of economic efficiency, use findings from the absorptive capacity theory, and can be applied to both evaluate existing environmental scanning systems and develop a new, more applicable generation. The findings should also be applicable to other IS domains.

Keywords Information systems (IS) analysis and design • Environmental scanning systems • Requirement analysis • Principle of economic efficiency • Absorptive capacity theory

---

An extended version of this article has been published as: Bischoff S, Weitzel T, Mayer JH (2012) Requirements criteria for applicable environmental scanning systems: model development and first demonstration. In: Mattfeld D, Robra-Bissantz S (eds) Proceedings der Multikonferenz Wirtschaftsinformatik 2012, Braunschweig, 29.02.2012. GITO, Berlin, pp 945–957.

S. Bischoff (✉)
University of St. Gallen, St. Gallen, Switzerland
e-mail: stefan.bischoff@unisg.ch

J.H. Mayer
School of Management, University of St. Gallen, St. Gallen, Switzerland
e-mail: joerg.mayer@unisg.ch

T. Weitzel • R. Quick
Darmstadt University of Technology, Darmstadt, Germany
e-mail: timm.weitzel@stud.tu darmstadt.de; quick@bwl.tu-darmstadt.de

J.H. Mayer, R. Quick (eds.), *Business Intelligence for New-Generation Managers*,
DOI 10.1007/978-3-319-15696-5_4

1 Introduction

The 2008/2009 economic crisis provided a sustainable impulse for focusing earlier on emerging threats and opportunities [20]. In particular, executives worry about not being prepared for environmental shifts or, even worse, not being able to parry them. *Environmental scanning*, ideally based on information systems (IS), can help to manage this challenge. Companies that do so will have brighter prospects.

With Ansoff's [2] article "Managing Strategic Surprise by Response to Weak Signals" as a flagship example, a substantial body of knowledge on this topic exists [3]. But, a lack of applicability means the concepts often go *unused* in practice [12]. A new examination of *requirements* with a focus on IS support can help to provide a starting point for developing more applicable environmental scanning systems.

This article contributes to better IS design by developing a *systematic list approach to requirements criteria* that specify the applicability of environmental scanning systems. Based on the principle of economic efficiency and using findings from the absorptive capacity theory, it can be applied to both evaluate existing environmental scanning systems and develop a new, more applicable generation.

We adhere to design science research in IS by developing innovative, generic solutions for practical problems [14]. Section 2 identifies current gaps in environmental scanning system design. In Sect. 3, we develop our list approach to requirements criteria. Section 4 discusses our model in terms of its applicability in a pilot study. Finally, Sect. 5 concludes the article with an outlook and proposal for further research.

2 Current Gaps in Environmental Scanning System Design

A company's environment could be defined as the relevant physical and social factors within and beyond the organization's boundaries [8]. While operational analysis focuses on (short-term) internal difficulties in the implementation of strategic programs, strategic environmental scanning aims at anticipating (long-term) environmental shifts and analyzing their potential impact [5]. This article concentrates on the latter, hereafter referred to as *environmental scanning*. As strategic issues can emerge within or outside a company, changes in both a company's external and internal environment are relevant. Thus, *environmental scanning systems* have to specify the sectors to be scanned, monitor the most important indicators of opportunities or threats for the company, cover the IS-based tools to be used, incorporate the findings of such analyses into decision making, and, often, assign responsibilities for supporting environmental scanning efforts (not covered in this article, but in [18]).

Requirements are defined as prerequisites, conditions or capabilities needed by users (individuals or systems) of a software system to solve a problem or achieve an objective [15]. Regarding a rigor requirements analysis, on the one hand, researchers work on *list approaches* dominated by a single principle: potential requirements are collected based on literature research or, most often, the authors'

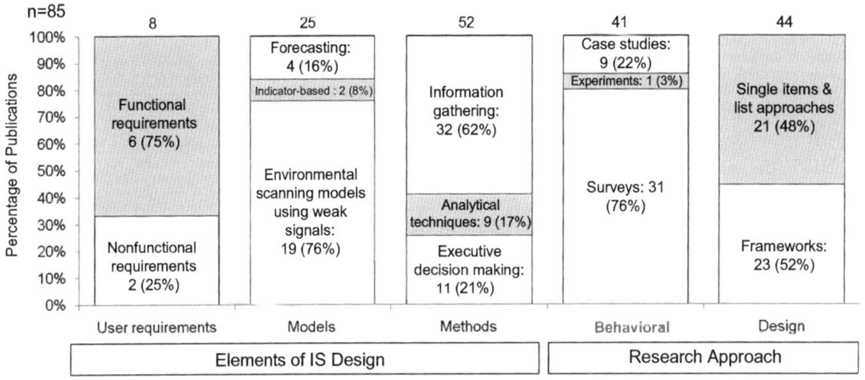

Fig. 1 Results of a current literature review [24]

own experience [23]. These approaches do not make use of an overall structuring principle or second-level structuring dimensions. Instead, the desire to be relevant for practice dominates the need for scientific rigor. On the other hand, behavioral IS research provides sound *structural models*. Examples are the DeLone and McLean IS success factors model [7] and the technology acceptance model (TAM) [6], however, in contrast to the list approaches, these are often not applicable in practice [32].

Our current literature review [24], revealed that out of 85 relevant publications, just eight examine requirements (Fig. 1): Most of them, such as Frolick et al. [11], follow just a simple list approach by mentioning several requirements without providing an overall structuring principle or second-level structuring dimensions. Other approaches are as diverse as the requirements they provide, and none apply a systematic process for developing requirements criteria (in detail [3], e.g., for the differentiation of model-free LoP, model-related LoR).

3 Model Development

The following sections on the model development are based on Bischoff et al. [3].

3.1 Principle of Economic Efficiency

We develop our model following Popper's approach [27], using deduction to define a systematic list to requirements criteria for environmental scanning systems. The principle of economic efficiency, which focuses on the ratio of cost and benefit, is a generally accepted paradigm in business research [28] and IS research [29]. It thus should serve as a good starting point for our model [3].

Principle of economic efficiency	Design criteria	Requirements criteria	
Solution capabilities (system output)	Information gathering	R1	Coverage of strategic risks (vision and strategic program)
		R2	Coverage of operational risks (internal and external value chain)
		R3	Coverage of information for "regulatory compliance"
		R4	Consideration of chances (adhering company-specific chance/risk ratio)
		R5	IS support: intensity and speed for information gathering
	Information interpretation	R6	Bias prevention
		R7	Level of knowledge and thinking process support
		R8	IS support: range of information interpretation
	Information usage	R9	Quality of information presentation
		R10	User interface and dialog control
		R11	Communication functionalities
		R12	IS support: ease of IS handling for information usage
	Cross-process factors	R13	Timeliness
		R14	Flexibility
		R15	Correctness (formal accuracy)
		R16	Reliability (accuracy in terms of content)
		R17	Level of interorganizational integration
		R18	IS support: IS transparency for cross-process factors
Resource requirements (system input)	Effort	R19	Cost adequacy
		R20	Time adequacy

Fig. 2 List approach to requirements criteria for applicable environmental scanning systems [3]

Even though the cost of IS design can be identified to some degree, quantifying the profitability of delivered information is limited. We express economic efficiency in a system of basic criteria (Fig. 2) and follow the "black box" method from mechanical engineering. These criteria can be differentiated into solution capabilities and resource requirements [22]. *Solution capabilities* cover how IS output supports environmental scanning for managers. The *resource requirements*, in turn, cover the input needed to generate the output.

3.2 First Level of Specification: Design Criteria

We follow Aguilar's [1] process-oriented view, and specify environmental scanning which gathers, interprets, and uses relevant information about events, trends, and relationships in an organization's environment. We start specifying solution capabilities for environmental scanning systems with *information gathering, interpretation and usage* capabilities as their design criteria. In addition, we suggest *cross-process factors* that contribute to capabilities not subsumed by the previous categories (Fig. 2). Resource requirements can be measured in terms of the *effort* to set up the environmental scanning system.

3.3 Second Level of Specification: Requirements Criteria

With respect to Aguilar's [1] definition, environmental scanning systems contribute to a company's absorptive capacity [35]. Thus, we examined research based on this theory to define our requirements criteria. Figure 2 illustrates our list approach to requirements criteria for specifying applicable environmental scanning systems. Taken from [3] we suggest as follows:

Information gathering A first objective for environmental scanning systems is to gather information concerning the company's vision and strategic program [4]. Because their direction is high-level and long term, we name the associated risks *strategic* ones (R1). Environmental scanning systems also have to incorporate a more short-term perspective. Regarding our definition (Sect. 2) we just focus on the most important *operational risks* relevant for management purpose. The scanning area is most often the company's internal and external value chain (R2). Furthermore, environmental scanning systems should focus on gathering information for "*regulatory compliance*" (R3) [23]. In addition to the most important risks, information gathering must take *chances* in a company-specific ratio into account [31] (R4). To sum it up, four criteria specifying the direction of information gathering for environmental scanning systems is the result: coverage of three types of *risks* (R1–R3) plus *chances* (R4).

Oh [26] finds evidence that leveraging "modern" IS capabilities (such as data mining, semantic search, and artificial neural networks) or collaboration techniques (such as RSS feeds, customer feedback on social media, professional databases [10]), or just business intelligence (BI) with a central data warehouse (DW) significantly enhances a company's process of information gathering [21, 26]. We summarize this perspective as "*IS support: intensity and speed for information gathering*" (R5).

Information interpretation Information interpretation covers the ability of IS to analyze and transform gathered information [35]. Following the bounded rationality theory information interpretation must take biased human cognition into account [25, 33]. Teece [31] argues that decision makers are biased in several forms. Innovations, for example, appear threatening for most human beings. Thus, adopting techniques to overcome these decision biases [31] can result in a competitive advantage. Jansen et al. [16] suggests involving more people in decision making, for example, having subordinates take part in higher-level decisions, and cross-functional interfaces as mechanisms. We summarize this in measuring *bias prevention* (R6).

Human attention becomes a scarce resource as the environment becomes more dynamic and complex [19]. Niu et al. [25] propose a "thinking support module" to provide a set of tools for knowledge management, including a case base and mental models or explicit and tacit knowledge. We thus define the *level of knowledge and thinking process support* as another criterion (R7).

From the IS support, March and Hevner [21] propose a data warehousing architecture with integration of external and internal data, as well as BI methods to interpret the information with respect to business. Niu et al. [25] mention online analytical processing (OLAP), SQL reporting, linear programming, and information fusion as methods for data analysis. Covering these aspects, we include the *range of information interpretation* (R8) as a next requirements criterion to our list approach.

Information usage Bearing in mind that managers still tend to be technology-averse and most often have a cognitive working style [17], the IS user interface is a key area determining IS acceptance. Following Warmouth and Yen [34], we evaluate the design of an environmental scanning system's user interface in three dimensions; *quality of information presentation* (R9), *user interface design* and *dialog control* (R10), and advanced functionalities managers can perform themselves. In terms of the latter, we concentrate on *communication functionalities* (R11). The *ease of IS handling* should help for a better information usage from IS perspective (R12).

Cross-process factors Cross-process factors contribute to several of the above-mentioned capabilities. First, the ability to adapt in time is of utmost importance in changing situations and turbulent environments [9]. Zott [36] defines *timeliness* as an important attribute of such dynamic capabilities (R13). We add *flexibility*, the ability of the IS to adapt to changing information needs, data sources, and ways to present information (R14). Managers will not use information if it is questionable in terms of its formal aspects or content [30]. This leads us to propose the requirements criteria of *correctness* (formal accuracy, R15) and *reliability* (accuracy in terms of content, R16).

Interorganizational factors, such as a company's social embeddedness, increase its absorptive capacity [26, 33]. Gulati [13] proposes that companies should "create and utilize wide-ranging information networks." Given the importance of networking activities, supporting companies' *level of interorganizational integration* is another requirements criterion for applicable environmental scanning systems (R17). Automatic validation checks are an example for IS support in the cross-process factors. Thus *IS transparency* should contribute to the cross-process factors (R18).

Effort Zott [36] states that "even if dynamic capabilities are equifinal across firms, robust performance may arise [...] if the costs and timing of dynamic capability deployment differ [...]." *Cost adequacy* (R19) and *time adequacy* (R20) are defined as the last requirements criteria.

4 Discussion

To evaluate the model proposed here, it was first implemented at a large international company (sales: US$56 bn; employees: 174,000). Comparing the findings with the comments from literature on IS list approaches and the structural models (Sect. 2) reveals that our model offers the following advantages (for details see Bischoff et al. [3]).

The principle of economic efficiency is widely *accepted* in both management and IS research. It should therefore provide a reliable design paradigm for structuring requirements analysis in general and designing environmental scanning systems design in particular, even for practitioners. Deriving design criteria from the findings of a theory such as absorptive capacity is scientifically *rigorous*. As we also included cross-functional IS aspects, our approach should lead to an acceptable level of *completeness and distinctiveness*.

Nonetheless, our list is *not exhaustive*. Founding environmental scanning in the theory of absorptive capacity is a new approach, and can prompt the criticism that using findings from a theory for evaluating applicability is a contradiction. But research about the antecedents of these theoretical constructs has been subject to surveys [33]. Compared with approaches based on the researcher's own experience or random literature, our model should be more *systematic* and *less subjective*.

5 Outlook and Future Research

The objective of this article was to contribute to better IS design by developing a systematic list approach to requirement criteria that specifies the applicability of environmental scanning systems. Based on the principle of economic efficiency and using findings from the absorptive capacity theory, we derived 20 requirements criteria. They can be applied to both evaluate existing environmental scanning systems and develop a new, more applicable generation.

Our list approach opens up opportunities for future research as it provides a first step to measure the applicability of company's environmental scanning systems in an efficient way. Overall, the results should be applicable to other IS domains as well and thus contribute to improved requirement analysis in IS design research in general.

References

1. Aguilar FJ (1967) Scanning the business environment. Macmillan, New York
2. Ansoff HI (1975) Managing strategic surprise by response to weak signals. Calif Manag Rev 18(2):21–33

3. Bischoff S, Weitzel T, Mayer JH (2012) Requirements criteria for applicable environmental scanning systems: model development and first demonstration. In: Mattfeld DC, Robra-Bissantz S (eds) Multikonferenz Wirtschaftsinformatik 2012 (MKWI 2012), Proceedings der Multikonferenz Wirtschaftsinformatik 2012. GITO Verlag, Braunschweig, pp 945–957
4. Committee of Sponsoring Organizations of the Treadway Commission (COSO) (2004) Enterprise risk management—integrated framework. COSO, New York
5. Davies J, Finlay M, McLenaghen T, Wilson D (2006) Key risk indicators—their role in operational risk management and measurement. In: Davis E (ed) The advanced measurement approach to operational risk. Risk Books, London, pp 215–246
6. Davis FD (1989) Perceived usefulness, perceived ease of use, and user acceptance of information technology. MIS Q 13(3):318–340
7. DeLone WH, McLean ER (2003) The DeLone and McLean model of information systems success: a ten-year update. J Manag Inform Syst 19(4):9–30
8. Duncan RB (1972) Characteristics of organizational environments and perceived environmental uncertainty. Admin Sci Q 17(3):313–327
9. Eisenhardt KM, Martin JA (2000) Dynamic capabilities: what are they? Strat Manag J 21 (10–11):1105–1121
10. Elofson G, Konsynski B (1991) Delegation technologies: environmental scanning with intelligent agents. J Manag Inform Syst 8(1):37–62
11. Frolick MN, Parzinger MJ, Rainer RKJ, Ramarapu N (1997) Using EISs for environmental scanning. Inform Syst Manag 14(1):35–40
12. Fuld L (2003) Be prepared. Harv Bus Rev 81(11):20–21
13. Gulati R, Nohria N, Zaheer A (2000) Strategic networks. Strat Manag J 21(3):203–215
14. Hevner AR, Chatterjee S (2010) Design research in information systems: theory and practice, vol 22, Integrated series in information systems. Springer, Berlin
15. IEEE (1998) IEEE recommended practice for software requirements specifications. Institute of Electrical & Electronics Engineers (IEEE) Computer Society, New York
16. Jansen JJP, Van Den Bosch FAJ, Volberda HW (2005) Managing potential and realized absorptive capacity: how do organizational antecedents matter? Acad Manag Rev 48 (6):999–1015
17. Jiang JJ, Muhanna WA, Klein G (2000) User resistance and strategies for promoting acceptance across system types. Inform Manag 37:25–36
18. Lenz RT, Engledow JL (1986) The applicability of current theory. Strat Manag J 7(4):329–346
19. Lipschitz R, Klein G, Orasanu J, Salas E (2001) Taking stock of naturalistic decision making. J Behav Decis Making 14:331–352
20. Makridakis S, Hogarth RM, Gaba A (2010) Why forecasts fail. What to do instead. MIT Sloan Manag Rev 51(2):83–90
21. March ST, Hevner AR (2007) Integrated decision support systems: a data warehousing perspective. Decis Support Syst 43(3):1031–1043
22. Matek W, Muhs D, Wittel H (1987) Maschinenelemente—Normung—Berechnung—Gestaltung. Vieweg, Braunschweig
23. Mayer JH, Marx F (2010) Systematic development of business-driven requirements—using next-generation EIS design as an example. In: Winter R, Zhao J, Aier S (eds) Fifth international conference on design science research in information systems and technology (DESRIST), St. Gallen, 4 June 2010. Springer, Heidelberg, pp 506–521
24. Mayer JH, Steinecke N (2011) Quick R improving the applicability of environmental scanning systems: state of the art and future research. In: Kautz K, Gadatsch A, Nüttgens M (eds) IFIP WG 8.6 working conference, Hamburg, 22–24 Sept 2011. Springer
25. Niu L, Lu J, Zhang G (2008) Cognitive orientation in business intelligence systems. Stud Comput Intell 117:55–72
26. Oh L-B (2009) Managing external information sources in digital extended enterprises: the role of IT enabled business intelligence competence and network structure strength. In: 30th international conference on information systems (ICIS), Phoenix, AZ, USA, pp 1–13

27. Popper KR (1982) Logik der Forschung, 7th edn. Mohr, Tübingen
28. Samuelson PA (1983) Foundations of economic analysis, Enlarged edition. Harvard University Press, Harvard, MA
29. Stair RM, Reynolds GW (2011) Principles of information systems, 10th edn. Course Technology, Boston, MA
30. Sutcliffe KM, Weber K (2003) The high cost of accurate knowledge. Harv Bus Rev 81 (5):74–82
31. Teece DJ (2007) Explicating dynamic capabilities: the nature and microfoundations of (sustainable) enterprise performance. Strat Manag J 28(8):1319–1350
32. Urbach N, Smolnik S, Riempp G (2009) The state of research on information systems success—a review of existing multidimensional approaches. Bus Inform Syst Eng 51 (4):315–325
33. Volberda HW, Foss NJ, Lyles MA (2010) Absorbing the concept of absorptive capacity: how to realize its potential in the organizational field. Organ Sci 21(4):931–951
34. Warmouth MT, Yen D (1992) A detailed analysis of executive information systems. Int J Inform Manag 12(2):192–208
35. Zahra SA, George G (2002) Absorptive capacity: a review, reconceptualization, and extension. Acad Manag Rev 27(2):185–203
36. Zott C (2003) Dynamic capabilities and the emergence of intra-industry differential firm performance: insights from a simulation study. Strat Manag J 24(1):97–125

Developing Individual IT-Enabled Capabilities for Management Control Systems

Janusch Patas

Abstract Management control systems (MCS) facilitate managers' decision making. At their core, MCS consist of corporate planning and reporting capabilities that rely on IT and non-IT assets. Recently, both researchers and practitioners have paid increasing attention to use maturity models (MM) for designing and using such capabilities effectively and efficiently. Although MMs are well-established and easy to apply, they lack a theoretical foundation and IS research focuses rather on their development process than on using them to create individual IT-enabled capabilities for MCS. We address this research gap by developing a method to systematically adjust MMs from the knowledge base to firm-specific business needs. Findings from the resource-based view (RBV) guide our development process. With an interpretative case study in the chemical sector we demonstrate the applicability of our method. We present a list of IT and non-IT assets that are necessary for our case company to develop individual IT-enabled planning and reporting capabilities. Information systems research benefits from our findings as we translate the RBV into action. Practice benefits from an individual view on their IT-enabled capabilities and we force managers to jointly consider their IT and non-IT assets when they are designing IT-enabled capabilities for their company.

Keywords Corporate Management • Management Control Systems • Resource-Based View • Maturity Models • IT-Enabled Capabilities • Method • Interpretative Case Study

1 Introduction

Increasing environmental volatility, new business models, and the globalization of organizations mean decision making is becoming more and more complex. In this environment, managers rely on *management control systems* (MCS) as they translate strategy into action and monitor the impact of these actions on their

J. Patas (✉)
Frankfurt School of Finance & Management, Frankfurt, Germany
e-mail: janusch.patas@gmx.de

J.H. Mayer, R. Quick (eds.), *Business Intelligence for New-Generation Managers*,
DOI 10.1007/978-3-319-15696-5_5

organization's performance [17]. At their core, MCS consist of an IT-enabled corporate planning and reporting system [2, 33].

Brynjolfsson and Hitt [7] emphasize the importance of leveraging *IT for business value* as follows: "Today, the critical question [...] managers are facing is not does IT pay off but how can we best use computers?" While researchers still debate on how to design IT-enabled planning and reporting capabilities that better address individual business needs [17, 23], IT management most often does not apply a systematic method to manage their resources, but rather follows software vendor promises or consultancy advices.

We propose a concept of *maturity models* (MM) to address this issue. Based on the stages of growth theory [40], they consist of multiple archetypal levels that represent the evolution of a certain domain [14]. In information systems (IS) MMs describe the extent to which a capability becomes more mature along a defined evolutionary path depending on the IT resources deployed. They can serve as powerful tool for designing and using IT effectively and efficiently [5].

MMs have increasingly gained the attention of both researchers and practitioners in recent years. Since the 1970s [9, 16], a variety of MMs has been developed. Becker et al. [5] reported more than 1,000 articles over a period of 15 years referring to MMs, and Mettler and Rohner [37] found more than 100 different versions from domains including knowledge management, project management, and business process management. Although MMs assess the current status of firm capabilities [48], there are two major points of criticism. First, MMs lack a *theoretical foundation* [45, 46]. To overcome this shortcoming we will use findings from the resource-based view (RBV) [4]. It is widely used in management research and provides researchers with a "robust framework for analyzing whether and how IT may be associated with competitive advantage" [36]. Second, Mettler and Rohner [37] found that MMs rarely provide firm-specific guidance on *how* to move from one maturity level to the next leveraging IT resources.

The objective of this chapter is therefore to develop a method to systematically adjust MMs from the knowledge base to firm-specific business needs, in our case, to finally arrive at individual *IT-enabled MCS capabilities*. We apply findings from the RBV to guide the development process of our method.

The chapter follows the tenets of design science research (DSR) in IS [21]. After a brief introduction of MCS we review the state of the art in MM research for MCS in order to identify the research gaps that motivate our method development (Sect. 2). We introduce the RBV as our design theory (Sect. 3.1) before we apply their findings to inform the development of our method (Sect. 3.2). Using an interpretive case study in the chemical sector we demonstrate how to adjust a MM from the knowledge base to develop the proposed firm-specific IT-enabled MCS capabilities (Sect. 4). Finally, we discuss our results before we lay out avenues for future research (Sect. 5).

2 Maturity Models for Management Control Systems

Corporate management formulates and implements value-creating strategies [8]. It thus encompasses formal instruments to coordinate and control an organization [2]. *MCS*, in turn, constitute such formal instruments, as they are defined as "formalized procedures and systems that use information to maintain or alter patterns in an organizational activity" [51]. The purpose of these systems is "to monitor decisions throughout the organization and to guide employee behavior in desirable ways in order to increase the chances that an organization's objectives, including organizational performance, will be achieved" [27]. Although research on MCS is predominantly driven by function, IT support is regarded as an important enabler [18].

As a measure of the effectiveness and efficiency of IS design and use, *maturity* can be defined as "the state of being complete, perfect or ready" [50] or, in a sense more specific to IS research, "a measure to evaluate the capabilities of an organization" [48]. A MM's scope is determined by its application domain and its focus area [53]. In order to specify the state of the art of MMs for MCS, we conducted a *literature review* according to vom Brocke et al. [56]. Using a keyword search in scientific literature databases, we first accessed EBSCOHost, SpringerLink, ABI/INFORM, and ScienceDirect. We limited our database search to title, abstract, and keywords. In a second iteration, we searched Google including MMs published in practitioner-oriented outlets. Our keywords covered both accounting information systems (AIS)-related as well as IS-related terms (Fig. 1).

After a closer look at the title, abstract, and keyword we identified 30 publications for an in-depth analysis. Studying the content of these papers, we examined *20 different MMs* for our analysis (Table 1). Ten papers were excluded due to the fact that they were lacking MMs or just described previously published ones. Our findings are presented in four main columns (1–4) where each column is decomposed into further dimensions. (1) MCS cover both planning and reporting as their most important capabilities; (2) To gather a wide range of MMs we searched the AIS in particular and the IS domains in general. (3) Most of the MMs origin in practice, not in research. (4) Finally, the column methodological support marks MMs if they provide the user with a method to adapt existing MMs.

MMs that address either planning or reporting are more or less equally covered in our findings. Furthermore, Table 1 shows that most MMs addressing MCS capabilities are developed in the IS and less in AIS domain. Moreover, the

‘AND‘	Stage model ‘OR‘ maturity model				
	Corporate management	Management control system	Planning ‘OR‘ corporate planning	Reporting ‘OR‘ corporate reporting	Corporate performance management
	AIS-related keywords			IS-related keywords	

Fig. 1 Search strings used for the structured literature review

Table 1 Maturity models for corporate management

	(1) MCS capabilities		(2) Domain		(3) Origin		(4) Method support
	Planning	Reporting	AIS	IS	Research	Practice	
[1]				✔	✔		
[3]	✔	✔	✔			✔	
[11]		✔	✔			✔	
[12, 13]				✔		✔	
[15]	✔	✔	✔			✔	
[19]	✔			✔	✔		
[20]	✔			✔		✔	
[22]				✔		✔	
[24]	✔	✔	✔			✔	
[25]	✔			✔		✔	
[26]		✔	✔		✔		
[28]	✔			✔		✔	
[29]	✔			✔	✔		
[32]	✔			✔	✔		
[35]		✔	✔		✔		
[38]				✔	✔		
[39]	✔	✔	✔			✔	
[49]				✔		✔	
[55]	✔			✔		✔	
[59]		✔	✔	✔	✔		

✔ = covered

examined MMs predominantly origin from practice as opposed to research. Thus, specifying our general criticism on MMs (Sect. 1), a first shortcoming of MMs addressing MCS capabilities is that they often lack a *theoretical foundation*. Furthermore, large chunks of MM research focus either on the (generic) development of MMs (e.g., [5]) or on the development process itself (e.g., [33]). We could neither find a single MM that provides a method that either guides the application and especially the adjustment of MMs to firm-specific business needs, nor the development of individual IT-enabled MCS capabilities. Existing MMs are often either too generic [11] or too specific [12]. Furthermore, our research indicates that MMs rarely provide prescriptive statements on how to advance from one maturity level to the next by leveraging IT resources.

We believe MCS and its MMs complement the "modern" AIS domain. If they are used to evaluate and design AIS, they provide a fact-driven evolvement of corporate management beyond "pure" state-of-the-art extrapolation. However, methodical support is required to raise their acceptance in general and in particular in AIS. Hence, this article introduces a method to systematically adjust MMs according to individual business needs to develop firm-specific IT-enabled, in our case, MCS capabilities.

3 Method Design

3.1 Design Theory

To overcome the shortcoming that MMs lack a formal theoretical foundation we follow Pöppelbuß et al. [46] who call for a theoretical foundation of MMs based on the RBV. The RBV states that every company consists of an individual bundle of resources [4]. The postulate of resource individuality, determining the uniqueness of every organization's resource combination, accounts for a probable sustainable competitive advantage. This comprehends two key propositions: First, resources are heterogeneous. Second, resources are immobile. Four attributes characterizes every resource: valuable (V), rare (R), inimitable (I), and non-substitutable (N)—VRIN. The peculiarities of these attributes determine the likelihood whether a resource is able to establish a (sustainable) competitive advantage [34]. In IS research, the RBV's core elements are *IT capabilities* (e.g. project management, programming) and (in-)tangible IT assets (e.g. hardware, software). *IT assets* are an input or output in a transformation process which is represented by (IT) capabilities [57]. As Nevo and Wade [41] have illustrated the combination of IT and non-IT assets form *IT-enabled capabilities*. Thus, the combination of both IT and non-IT assets is a prerequisite to enable organizational capabilities with IT.

Patas [42] made a first attempt to base the MM concept and its components in theory. Using the RBV he converts basic MM components into RBV elements as depictured in Fig. 2. A MM's structure is typically based on the Capability Maturity Model (CMM) for Software Engineering. According to Fraser et al. [14], MMs usually define a number of maturity levels, a concise descriptor for each level, a description of the content of each level, several dimensions to concentrate on a certain domain aspect (e.g., corporate planning in corporate management), and a set of elements and activities (e.g., knowledge, business practices, software, hardware, etc.) for each level. MMs should also encompass an assessment instrument, usually in form and function of a questionnaire that helps to evaluate the current maturity level of a capability [33].

The most basic elements of the RBV are IT assets and non-IT assets transformed into IT-enabled capabilities. *Elements* and *activities* are the most granular MM components defined at each maturity level within a dimension. We therefore

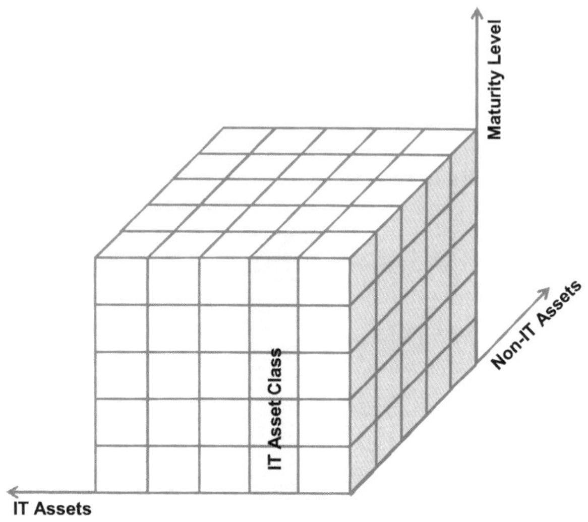

Fig. 2 Maturity model cube

convert elements and activities into the constructs assets (both tangible or intangible and IT or non-IT) and dimension into the construct IT-enabled capabilities. While dimensions were able to cover, for instance, solely IT elements such as software and hardware, now capabilities require a combination of IT and non-IT assets to be considered IT-enabled. The MM component focus area expresses a certain class of non-IT or IT assets. We convert focus area into the construct asset class to reflect a stream of assets evolving along the determined IT-enabled capability evolution path. In this course, we leave generic description of maturity level and level descriptor unchanged as the RBV defines no equivalents. However, they constitute some descriptive constructs that are required for the MM documentation. Figure 2 shows the relations of the constructs that form the so-called MM cube.

The MM cube shows the maturation path for a single IT-enabled capability (e.g., IT-enabled corporate reporting). We decided to depict five levels on the MM cube because MMs generally define five levels [37]. IT assets are located on the x-axis and non-IT assets on the z-axis. The y-axis represents the maturation path based on the stages hypothesis. Every single elementary cube represents a combination of IT and non-IT assets on a particular maturity level. Slicing the cube horizontally returns an IT-enabled capability layer that shows all IT and non-IT assets and their combinations on a particular maturity level. Slicing this cube vertically returns the maturation path for a single asset class showing all possible combinations with either IT or non-IT assets.

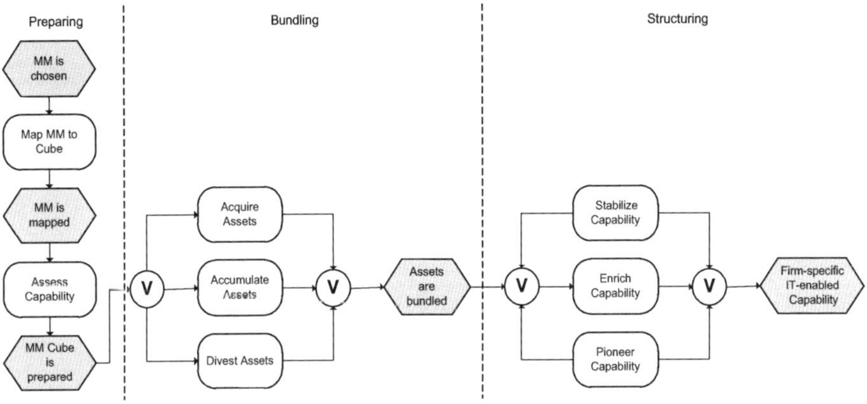

Fig. 3 Adjusting MMs to individual business needs to build firm-specific IT-enabled capabilities

3.2 Constructing the Method

We adopt the process framework proposed by Sirmon et al. [52] to structure and bundle resources before the capabilities are deployed. Once again, each of those three processes is divided into three sub processes. We intend our method to be applied according to March and Smith [31] as "... way of performing goal-directed activities..." in order to adjust MMs from the knowledge base to firm-specific business needs with the goal to develop individual IT-enabled capabilities. Therefore, we complement our method with a preparing process. Subsequently we describe the entire method consisting of the three main processes preparing, bundling, and structuring as illustrated in Fig. 3.

Preparing comprises the two sub processes mapping, and assessing. *Mapping* projects the selected MM on the MM cube in order to prepare it for subsequent adjustments. Therefore, the chosen MM has to be first analyzed in order to map the relevant components (assets classes, IT assets, non-IT assets, etc.) to the MM cube. If the mapping sub process reveals that, for instance, the selected MM provides no IT assets or no non-IT assets, another MM might be more appropriate or the current MM has to be extended within the following sub processes. Subsequently, *assessing* the as-is situation returns the current maturity level and the missing assets in the organization's portfolio according to the MM cube.

Structuring the asset portfolio consists of the three sub processes acquiring, accumulating, and divesting, whereby not all sub processes have to be necessarily carried out. To close the asset gaps revealed during the assessment, two sub processes are suggested. While *acquiring* refers to deciding whether the missing assets have to be bought, *accumulating* deals with the question whether those assets should be better engineered. More clearly, make or by decisions have to be made. Finally, *divesting* decisions are required. On the one hand, some assets might be out-of-date and are therefore not state-of-the-art technologies. On the other hand, some assets might be very expensive in their maintenance. Therefore, an analysis from an economic perspective should reveal divestment opportunities when this process step is performed [47].

Bundling deals with developing or altering IT-enabled capabilities. It is detailed by the following disjunctive non mutual exclusive sub processes stabilizing, enriching, and pioneering. *Stabilizing* refers to minor changes and improvements on an IT-enabled capability to keep it "up-to-date" by changing some parameters of an elementary cube; for instance, training an employee in its current working domain. *Enriching* refers to the extension or elaboration of an existing IT-enabled capability. This sub process can be accomplished with a dicing operation. For example, enriching refers to extending a software application with new modules (SAP extended with SAP CRM). Regarding *pioneering*, Sirmon et al. [52] emphasize that it "... may involve the integration of completely new resources that were recently acquired from strategic factor markets and added to the firm's resource portfolio." If only non-IT assets are mapped to a MM cube, the capability has to be redesigned by incorporating IT asset classes to form firm-specific IT-enabled capabilities.

4 Demonstrating the Method

4.1 Research Design

Demonstrating the applicability of an IS artifact is an important activity in DSR in IS [21]. Peffers et al. [44] consider *case studies* as an appropriate method to accomplish this task. Case studies are recommended to answer "how" or "why" questions [58, 60]. As we focus on "how" our method works in practice, we demonstrate that it can be used to systematically adjust MMs from the knowledge base to individual business needs with the goal to finally develop firm-specific IT-enabled capabilities (Sect. 1).

We studied three organizations in the Chemical sector that were merged into a *joint venture* (JV) during our research period from October 2011 to March 2012. The management board decided to design a new organization including the IT infrastructure, business processes, compensation systems, etc. They were curios whether our method can be applied to analyze corporate management's agenda covering the design and development of IT-enabled corporate planning and reporting capabilities. Based on our findings, the companies' benefits were an assessment of the as-is situation using a MM for MCSs before the JV was formed. Additionally we provided them with an evaluation of their transformation agenda to establish and design IT-enabled planning and reporting capabilities.

4.2 Case Setting, Data Collection and Analysis

Before entering the field, Darke et al. [10] recommend specifying the constructs that are going to be demonstrated. Besides maturity level descriptor, generic maturity level description, and IT-enabled capabilities, our constructs cover IT and non-IT assets as well as asset classes. To instantiate our method we have specified a prior IT and non-IT asset classes taken from Patas et al. [43]. In so doing, we "[. . .] create [d] a framework which takes account of previous knowledge [. . .]" [58]. In detail, the IT asset (ITA) classes are: technological assets (ITA1), e.g. hardware and software; technological quality assets (ITA2), e.g., modularity, availability, security; IT external relationship assets (ITA3), e.g., information sharing with customers and suppliers. Non-IT asset classes are human assets (NIT1), e.g., cooperation, ability to learn, enthusiasm, skills; knowledge assets (NIT2), e.g., business process knowledge; business assets (NIT3), e.g., business work practices and templates, key performance indicators, strategies. Specifying constructs before entering the field helped us to analyze whether planning and reporting capabilities are designed to qualify as IT-enabled.

Located in Europe, *Organization A* was a large division of a listed group with revenues of approx. €3.7 bn. It had more than 1,400 employees and produced styrene plastics. *Organization B*, employing about 1,200 people with revenues of about € 2.1 bn., was also located in Europe and produced ethylbenzene and styrene monomer. *Organization C* specialized in the production of synthetic terpolymers was located in the United States. Although it employed more than 1,500 people, in terms of revenues (0.8 bn.) it was the smallest organization. The new JV is located in Europe with about 6.5 bn. revenues and with more than 3,100 employees. Notably, as it mainly sells commodities it acts in a volatile environment with volatile prices but has also some R&D (Table 2).

For data collection we used multiple sources as recommended in Yin [60] and documented in Table 3. Data collection was conducted from October 2011 to March 2012. Two researchers were involved, including an assistant professor and a doctoral student in the end of his third year.

4.3 Instantiating the Method

Preparing

Within selecting we chose the KPMG corporate performance management MM summarized in Table 4 for two reasons. First, it is used in practice, but was developed rigorously in collaboration with academia. All maturity levels are empirically derived using the Rasch algorithm [33]. Second, in contrast to the majority of published maturity models, it comes with an assessment instruments that we applied to evaluate the as-is situation before the JV was formed.

Table 2 Key figures prior to and after forming the JV

	Organizations ex-ante to JV		
	Organization A	Organization B	Organization C
Employees	1,400	1,200	1,500
Revenues	€3.7 bn.	€2.1 bn.	€0.8 bn.
Headquarter	Europe	Europe	United States
Reporting: as-is	Level 4: Strategy-driven	Level 2: Guided	Level 3: Integrated
Planning: as-is	Level 3: Integrated	Level 2: Guided	Level 3: Integrated
	Ex-post: JV		
Revenues		€6.5 bn.	
Employees		3,100	

Table 3 Data sources and methods

Data sources	Description
Semi-structured Interviews	As-is assessment of Organization A and elicitation IT and non-IT assets One interview with JV's project coordinator corporate planning and reporting for 60 min using the assessment instrument and a questionnaire One interview with ex-ante and ex-post member of global controlling for 60 min using the assessment instrument and a questionnaire As-is assessment of Organization B and elicitation of IT and non-IT assets One telephone interview with ex-ante global controller and ex-post member of EMEA controlling for 60 min using the assessment instrument and a questionnaire As-is assessment of Organization C and elicitation of IT and non-IT assets One telephone interview with ex-ante global controller and ex-post head of region EMEA for 60 min using the assessment instrument and a questionnaire
Observations	Participating in strategic meetings, informal talks with CEO, CFO, Head of Global Controlling, Global Controllers, IT management, IT project managers, and consultants
Archival documents	Studying and analyzing documents of ex-ante IT architecture, business processes, KPI reports, budgeting processes and other business processes
Group discussion	Results discussion with project leader corporate planning and reporting JV, IT management, and IT project management

The MM summarized in Table 4 has no defined IT and non IT-asset classes. Mapping the MM to the MM cube requires first to elicit necessary assets both for planning as well as reporting capabilities on every maturity level. We used semi-structured interviews, described in Table 3, and asked four interviewees about instances of our pre-specified constructs for each maturity level and we briefly assessed the as-is situation to gather background information about the pre-JV situation. The two researchers jointly conducted the interviews. After summarizing the outcomes, removing repeatedly mentioned assets, generalizing the assets (for instance, replacing SAP ERP by the system class ERP systems), and comparing

Table 4 MM for corporate planning and reporting capabilities [28]

MM level descriptor		Corporate planning capability	Corporate reporting capability
Level 1: Basic	Generic Description of Maturity Level	Short-term planning is primary financially oriented. It is prepared manually using spreadsheets	Reporting is oriented towards financial measures and external requirements. The focus is on executives and the process is highly manual, resulting in paper-based standard reports
Level 2: Guided		Long-term planning is supported by planning systems [as well], but not aligned with operational planning. Therefore, planning quality is moderate, as planning methods and IT support are basic	Extended management approach with focus on additional internal management requirements, which leads to reporting and analysis services for corporate and business units
Level 3: Integrated		Comprehensive financially oriented planning systems based on well-organized planning processes. Templates are established. A concept-oriented planning application is used	Comprehensive reporting approach with [additional] risk and compliance measures, advanced analysis, and dedicated services for specific user groups. It is based on well designed and automated reporting processes, advanced analysis tools, and information portals
Level 4: Strategy-driven		Long-term and short-term planning support for the organization vision and strategic program and are linked [to each other]. Advanced IT makes it possible to relieve management accounting of basic tasks and supports its new role as a business partner	Reporting approaches emphasizes strategic measures, analysis, and instruments. Management accounting is relieved of standard reporting tasks and shifts towards the role of a business partner
Level 5: IT-advanced		Corporate planning leverages the potential of modern IT support for process optimization, planning integration, and enhanced quality	Reporting approach leverages the potential of modern IT systems. Executives are "self-empowered" with mobile devices and dashboards

them with the MM, we returned the results to our interviewees asking for comments. As they did not come up with change requests, we mapped the assets to the MM cube (Fig. 4). The next sub process, *assessing the JV's as-is situation*, was straight forward. Due to the early situation of the JV and the decision to design a completely new organization from scratch, only five figures were reported to the management board on global and on regions level and virtually no planning was

Non-IT ASSETS (NIT)	Maturity Level		Corporate Planning Capabilities			Corporate Reporting Capabilities		
			NIT1 – Human	NIT1 – Knowledge	NIT1 – Business	NIT1 – Human	NIT1 – Knowledge	NIT1 – Business
	L1	Basic	Not IT-averse, sufficient working skills and experience in manual tasks, enough employees for data collection	General knowledge about planning KPIs, about raw material prices and price trends, basic knowledge on financial KPIs	Basic understanding of value chain	Not IT-averse	Basic skills in office applications, KPI knowledge	Basic sector KPIs, simple business analyses
	L2	Guided	IT affinity, sufficient working skills, ability to work in teams, communication and coordination skills, work experience	Advanced Knowledge about planning KPIs, raw material prices and price trends	Simulation routine, markets development analyses, integrated long- and short-term planning	Explication of business needs, communication and coordination skills, ability to work in teams, sufficient experienced accountants in manual working tasks	Cross-application skills in office applications, KPI knowledge with some years of implementation experience	Documented KPIs, defined reporting standards from management board, comments on KPI deviations
	L3	Integrated	Communication and coordination skills with customers, assertiveness, responsibility, basic leadership, willing to continual educate	Knowledge about planning relations and problems, core business knowledge	Reconciliation of sub plans with planning process, contact with customers to plan raw material, business analyses	Training for non-accountants in accounting fundamentals, communication skills in different business fields	Non accountants have knowledge how to generate reports, knowledge about industrial sector and customers, business knowledge	Involved departments have fundamental understanding of KPIs, good business relations with suppliers/customers, Risk/Compliance KPIs
	L4	Strategy-driven	Cooperation skills, information sharing, team leading capabilities, IT/business partnering, strategic thinking, consulting ability	Knowledge and understanding about strategic plans, about new markets and production processes	Involvement of all accountants in planning/information sharing, economic models of market developments, business partnering	Skills in innovation and project management, accountants act as business partners, communication with executives, experience with different IS	Knowledge in other management accounting disciplines, in-deep business knowledge, deep application knowledge including query building	Reporting for projects and innovations, master data management, business partnering,
	L5	IT-advanced	Acceptance of new technology, willingness to learn	Ad-hoc analysis knowledge and about workflow software, knowledge about design for use	Well documented sector-specific planning process	Acceptance of different information channel and mobile devices on top management level, information security awareness	Knowledge about usage of mobile devices, design for use, ad-hoc queries, navigation skills in reporting tools	User-specific reports also on mobiles devices, in-deep business analyses

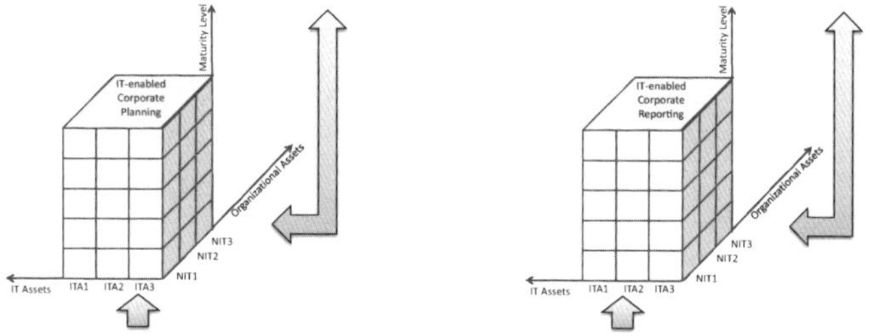

IT ASSETS (ITA)	Maturity Level		Corporate Planning Capabilities			Corporate Reporting Capabilities		
			ITA1 – Technological	ITA1 – Technological Quality	ITA1 – IT External Relationship	ITA1 – Technological	ITA1 – Technological Quality	ITA1 – IT External Relationship
	L1	Basic	Flat spreadsheets	Easy to use tools, cost efficiency	Collecting information from external information suppliers	Flat spreadsheets	Easy access, short response time, easy to understand and use	
	L2	Guided	Spreadsheets with simple forecast, simple databases, comprehensive office packages	Easy customizable tools, simulation routines, validity checks, persistent an available historical data	Assumptions about market trends and developments, market intelligence	Simple database	Availability of historical data, cost efficiency	
	L3	Integrated	Planning application	Integrated and consistent data, short response time, availability, role-based access rights, automated and interlinked spreadsheets	Access to planning tools via intranet, online request of raw materials prices from suppliers	Data warehouse, advanced spreadsheets, ERP systems	Multidimensional data models, role models, high-performance historical data storage and access	Role models for distribution of reports via intranet
	L4	Strategy-driven	Identity management system, tool support for simulation of strategic decisions, integrated planning system	Role-based access to strategic data, easy implementation of strategic data, integrated data (self-checking)	Role models for distribution and access of information via intranet	BI tools, dash boards	Visualization of KPIs, manageable user authorization, usability, cost efficiency, defined master data	Automated integration of external information provider, Role models to access management reports via intranet
	L5	IT-advanced	Workflow management system, integrated office tools with ERP systems	Ad-hoc analysis of planning data, automation of services, reduced amount of different applications	Predefined ad-hoc queries available via intranet	Push reporting software, mobile devices	Adjusted reports for mobile devices, ad-hoc analysis, usability and easy navigation	Mobile availability of information, external access to management reports

Fig. 4 Conceptualization of the results and their mapping to the MM cube

carried out until January 2012. Although, according to Fig. 4 some assets were already deployed, we evaluated the as-is situation at L0 of both planning and reporting.

Structuring

According to the *structuring process*, management made different decisions that fit into the sub processes *acquiring, accumulating, and divesting*. For instance, most IT technological assets (ITA1) can be *acquired* from the factors market. Hereunto, the JV's management board planned to roll out a standard ERP system, a data warehouse, as well as advanced BI analytics including a dashboard. They planned to enable their planning and reporting capabilities with IT over the next 2 years. Conversely, *accumulating* refers to assets that are hard to acquire; thus, assets that have to be developed. Analyzing the pre-JV situation for planning and reporting, the JV owns very diverse non-IT assets. With respect to their reporting capabilities, they were not lacking human, knowledge, and business assets evaluated at L4. However, we observed a broad variety of maturity levels within the asset classes. For instance, in Organization A accountants were acting as business partners. They have experience in communicating with the board and also know how to formulate data queries using advanced BI tools. *Divesting* decisions were also made. The three organizations were running seven different ERP system instances in total. To overcome the disadvantageous heterogeneity in their IT architecture, the board decided to acquire a state of the art system instead of facing the effort related to integration tasks and the corresponding political issues.

Bundling

Depending on the actual case the decision has to be made whether one or all three sub processes have to be carried out [52]. In the JV case, *stabilizing* is not reasonable, as incremental improvements require the existence of IT-enabled planning or reporting capabilities. However, we found indicators that the management tried to *enrich* their capabilities. For instance, on global and regions level the management accounting department formed groups consisting of accounting employees from all three pre JV organizations. The goal was to improve the non-IT assets NIT1, NIT2, and NIT3, classified on lower maturity level by mixing them with the more advanced assets for IT-enabled planning and reporting. Workshops were also organized to support this goal.

Pioneering entails a major challenge especially in the situation of forming a JV when new resources have to be incorporated. According to the project plan, the JV aspired to achieve maturity level L4 regarding their IT assets. However, our analysis revealed that management had no clear vision how to build unique IT-enabled planning and reporting capabilities. The project plan was mainly concerned with the implementation of IT assets completely disregarding non-IT assets. In contrast, the MM cube suggests combining and integrating IT and non-IT assets to form firm-specific IT-enabled planning and reporting capabilities (Fig. 4).

5 Conclusion, Limitations and Future Research

The objective of this chapter was to develop a method to systematically adjust MMs from the knowledge base to firm-specific business needs to form IT-enabled capabilities. Using a MM for MCS, we demonstrated how to apply our method and how to provide management with an individual view on their IT assets and non-IT assets. Our contribution to *research* is twofold. First, while research most often deals with the MM development itself, we introduced a method adjusting MMs to develop firm-specific IT-enabled capabilities. Second, we demonstrated how the RBV can be translated into action. *Practice* benefits from our findings as we introduce a comprehensive view on organizations' IT-enabled capabilities and force managers to jointly consider their IT and non-IT assets according to their individual business needs. In this respect, managers can choose a MM that fits best their needs and adjust it in order to design firm-specific IT-enabled capabilities.

Shortcomings are that our approach does not constitute a comprehensive method according to method engineering. We do not define components such as roles, techniques, meta model, results, or tools [6]. Particularly, techniques could be valuable to support the different sub processes such as mapping or divesting decisions. Furthermore, we only demonstrated how to adjust one MM and then analyzed the suitability of the method to develop firm-specific IT-enabled capabilities. We did not evaluated whether our model will work with other MMs as well. In future research our method needs to be extended towards its comprehensiveness to support MM adjustments without any ambiguity. Moreover, as the RBV is associated with firm performance and competitive advantage, our approach could be studied under the light of IT business value or even the dynamic capability view [54].

References

1. Aho M (2009) A capability maturity model for corporate performance management – an empirical study in large Finnish companies, Jyväskylä
2. Anthony RN, Govindarajan V (2006) Management control systems. McGraw-Hill, New York
3. Arveson P, Rohm H, Wilsey D, Perry G, Halbach L, DeCarlo J (2010) The strategic management maturity model. Balanced Scorecard Institute, Cary, North Carolina
4. Barney J (1991) Firm resources and sustained competitive advantage. J Manag 17(1):99–120
5. Becker J, Knackstedt R, Pöppelbuß J (2009) Developing maturity models for IT management—a procedure model and its application. Bus Inform Syst Eng 1(3):213–222
6. Brinkkemper S (1996) Method engineering: engineering of information systems development methods and tools. Inform Manag 38(2):275–280
7. Brynjolfsson E, Hitt LM (1998) Beyond the productivity paradox. CACM 41(8):49–55
8. Collis DJ, Montgomery CA (1998) Corporate strategy—a resource-based approach. McGraw-Hill, New York
9. Crosby PB (1979) Quality is free—the art of making quality certain. McGraw-Hill, New York
10. Darke P, Shanks G, Broadbent M (1998) Successfully completing case study research: combining rigour, relevance and pragmatism. Inform Syst J 8(4):273–289
11. Deloitte (2011) Integrated reporting—a better view? http://deloitte.com/assets/Dcom-GlobalLocal%20Assets/Documents/Sustainability%20and%20Climate%20Change/dttlDeloitte_Integrated_reporting_a_better_views_Sept_2011.2.pdf. Accessed 6 Nov 2011
12. Eckerson W (2004) Gauge your data warehousing maturity. DM Review. http://www.information-management.com/issues/20041101/1012391-1.html. Accessed 1 Nov 2012
13. Eckerson WW, Howson C (2005) Enterprise BI: strategies and technologies for deploying BI on an Enterprise scale, TDWI report series, The Data Warehouse Institute. http://www.tdwi.org

14. Fraser P, Moultrie J, Gregory M (2002) The use of models/grids as a tool in assessing product development capability. Paper presented at the IEEE international engineering management conference, Cambridge
15. Gluck FW, Kaufmann SP, Walleck SA (1980) Strategic management for competitive advantage. HBR 58:154–161
16. Gibson CF, Nolan RL (1974) Managing the four stages of EDP growth. HBR 52(1):76–88
17. Granlund M (2011) Extending AIS research to management accounting and control issues: a research note. Int J Account Inform Syst 12(1):3–19
18. Granlund MT, Malmi T (2002) Moderate impact of ERPS on management accounting: a lag or permanent outcome? Manag Account Res 13(3):299–321
19. Grover V, Segars AH (2005) An evaluation of stages of strategic information systems planning: patterns of process design and effectiveness. Inform Manag 42(5):761–779
20. Heer R (2011) The planning maturity curve: where are you? Where do you want to be? Alight research paper. http://www.alightplanning.com/downloads/The_Planning_Maturity_Curve.pdf
21. Hevner AR, March S, Park J, Ram S (2004) Design science in information systems research. MIS Q 28(1):75–105
22. Hewlett-Packard (2001) Describing the BI journey: the HP business intelligence (BI) maturity model. http://www8.hp.com/h20195/v2/GetPDF.aspx%2F4AA3-9723EEW.pdf
23. Hopwood AG (2009) The economic crisis and accounting: implications for the research community. Account Org Soc 34(6/7):797–802
24. International Federation of Accountants – IFAC (2009) Evaluating and improving costing in organizations. International Good Practice Guidance, New York
25. IT Governance Institut (2007) CobiT 4.1. www.itgi.org
26. Kaplan RS (1990) The four-stage model of cost systems. Manag Account 8:22–26
27. Kallunki JP, Laitinen EK, Silvola H (2011) Impact of enterprise resource planning systems on management control systems and firm performance. Int J Account Inform Syst 12(1):20–39
28. KPMG (2011) Reifegrade im corporate performance management. http://www.kpmg.de/media/corporate-performance-management-20110909.pdf. Accessed 6 Nov 2012
29. Lapide L (2005) An S&OP maturity model. J Bus Forecast, Fall, 2005
30. Maier AM, Moultrie J, Clarkson PJ (2009) Developing maturity grids for assessing organisational capabilities: practitioner guidance. In: 4th international conference on MCD, Italy, Vienna
31. March S, Smith G (1995) Design and natural science research on information technology. Decis Support Syst 15(4):251–266
32. Marx F, Lahrmann G, Winter R (2010) Aligning corporate planning and BI: towards a combined maturity model. In: 7th conference of the Italian chapter of AIS (itAIS 2010), Naples
33. Marx F, Wortmann F, Mayer JH (2012) A maturity model for management control systems. Bus Inform Syst Eng 4(4):193–207
34. Mata FJ, Fuerst WJ, Barney JB (1995) Information technology and sustained competitive advantage: a resource based analysis. MIS Q 19(4):487–505
35. McRoberts HA, Sloan BC (1998) Financial management capability model. Int J Gov Audit 25 (3):8–11
36. Melville M, Kraemer K, Gurbaxani V (2004) Information technology and organizational performance: an integrative model of IT business value. MIS Q 28(2):283–322
37. Mettler T, Rohner P (2009) Situational maturity models as instrumental artifacts for organizational design. In: Proceedings of the 4th international conference on design science research in information systems and technology, New York, pp 1–9
38. Muntean M, Bologa AR, Bologa R, Florea A (2011) The use of multidimensional models to increase the efficiency of management support systems. IJM3AS 8(5):1334–1344
39. National-Audit-Office (2010) Financial management maturity model. http://www.nao.org.uk/help_for_public_services/financial_management/fmmm.aspx
40. Nolan R (1973) Managing the computer resource: a stage hypothesis. CACM 16(7):399–405

41. Nevo S, Wade M (2011) Firm-level benefits of IT-enabled resources: a conceptual extension and an empirical assessment. J Strat Inform Syst 20(4):403–418
42. Patas J (2012) Towards maturity models as methods to manage IT for business value—a resource-based view foundation. In: Proceedings of the 18th American conference on information systems, Lima, pp 1–9
43. Patas J, Bartenschlager J, Goeken M (2012) Resource-based view in empirical IT business value research—an evidence-based literature review. In: Proceedings of the 45th Hawaii international conference on system science, Maui, pp 5062–5071
44. Peffers K, Tuunanen T, Rothenberger M, Chatterjee S (2007) A design science research methodology for information systems research. JMIS 24(3):45–78
45. Pöppelbuß J, Rögglinger M (2011) What makes a useful maturity model? A framework of general design principles for maturity models and its demonstration in business process management. In: Proceedings of the 19th European conference on information systems, Helsinki, pp 1–12
46. Pöppelbuß J, Niehaves B, Simons A, Becker J (2011) Maturity models in information systems research: literature search and analysis. CAIS 29(1):1–15
47. Röglinger M, Kamprath N (2011) Prozessverbesserung mit Reifegradmodellen—Eine Analyse ökonomischer Zusammenhänge. Zeitschrift für Betriebswirtschaft 52(5):509–538
48. Rosemann M, De Bruin T (2005) Towards a business process management maturity model. In: Proceedings of the 13th European conference on information systems, Regensburg, pp 1–12
49. Schulze KL, Dittmar C (2006) Business Intelligence Reifegradmodelle. In: Chamoni P, Gluchowski P (eds) Analytische Informationssysteme. Springer, Berlin, pp 71–87
50. Simpson JA, Weiner ESC (1989) The Oxford English dictionary. Oxford University Press, Oxford
51. Simons R (1987) Accounting control systems and business strategy: an empirical analysis. Account Org Soc 12(4):357–374
52. Sirmon DG, Hitt MA, Ireland RD (2007) Managing firm resources in dynamic environments to create value: looking inside the black box. Acad Manag Rev 32(1):273–292
53. Steenbergen M, Bos R, Brinkkemper S, Weerd I, Bekkers W (2010) The design of focus area maturity models. In: Proceedings of the 5th international conference on design science research in information systems and technology, St. Gallen, pp 317–332
54. Teece D, Pisano G, Shuen A (1997) Dynamic capabilities and strategic management. Strat Manag J 18(7):509–533
55. Thiruvenkatachari BS, Kartick R (2009) Corporate performance management – maturity model approach, Satyam
56. vom Brocke J, Simons A, Niehaves B, Riemer K, Plattfaut R, Cleven A (2009) Reconstructing the giant: on the importance of rigour in documenting the literature search process. In: Proceedings of the 17th European conference on information systems, Verona, pp 1–13
57. Wade M, Hulland J (2004) The resource-based view and information systems research: review, extension, and suggestions for future research. MIS Q 28(1):107–142
58. Walsham G (1995) Interpretive case studies in IS research: nature and method. Eur J Inform Syst 4(2):74–81
59. Wettstein T, Kueng P (2002) A maturity model for performance measurement systems. In: Brebbia CA, Pascolo P (eds) Management information systems 2002: GIS and remote sensing. WIT Press, Southampton
60. Yin RK (2009) Case study research: design and method. SAGE, Thousand Oaks

Towards an Evaluation Framework to Structure Business Intelligence Project Patterns as Enhancement of Business Intelligence Maturity Models

Carsten Felden, Claudia Koschtial, and Peter Chamoni

Abstract Maturity models are introduced to support the evaluation of the status quo of IT inside a company and to identify next applicable steps, but it has been revealed that Business Intelligence (BI) maturity models are still in a learning phase so far. Existing models are not mainly based within practical environment, yet, so that the positioning of the own company's status quo and comparison to competitors does not help in decision making in context of next steps in BI investments. We are analyzing several existing BI project descriptions, which were part of the *TDWI BI Best Practice Award*, to be able to contribute to the discussion of BI project definitions. Project patterns are identified, which are organized in a blueprint. This result serves as a first step and road sign towards a scalable BI management support, to increase the discussion about maturity models and to support BI strategies and investment decisions for project definitions.

Keywords Business Intelligence • BI Governance • BI Strategy

1 Introduction

Hence the need for a Business Intelligence (BI) strategy is known in most companies, just 12 % of German companies have implemented a BI strategy, 40 % are in the process of implementation whereas 17 % have only planned to do so. 31 % of companies do not have a specific BI strategy but a general IT strategy. There is also a trend towards BI specific organizations (like BI Competence Centers, BICC): In 2006 there were 65 % of companies lacking a professional BI organization. In 2009

C. Felden (✉) • C. Koschtial
Technische Universität Bergakademie Freiberg, Freiberg, Germany
e-mail: carsten.felden@bwl.tu-freiberg.de; claudia.koschtial@bwl.tu-freiberg.de

P. Chamoni
Universität Duisburg-Essen, Duisburg, Germany
e-mail: peter.chamoni@uni-duc.de

J.H. Mayer, R. Quick (eds.), *Business Intelligence for New-Generation Managers*,
DOI 10.1007/978-3-319-15696-5_6

the percentage decreased to 38 % [11]. This chapter analyzes the history of BI culminating to the development for a BI management support. It is the chapter's goal to set a framework based on BI project patterns to be able to evaluate company's own status quo and to be able to position it in relation to competitors.

Maturity models offer orientation for BI projects. Additionally, they are also used to evaluate implementations from an external viewpoint. One of the very first BI maturity models was built on project experience and best practice. One comprehensive approach to such governance is the Business Intelligence Maturity Model, others and more general ones are CObIT, CMMI, or ITIL which group activities into processes.[1] All frameworks recognize that there is a number of dimensions or attributes of maturity. As a management task, target maturity levels are expected to vary for different individual BI strategies (if existent), BI processes, BI infrastructure, and industry characteristics. Differences in maturity come from factors such as risks facing the organization and the contribution of processes to value generation and service delivery. BI managers must pose the question: Where should we be for our key activities? Or, at least: How do we compare to our peers? Unfortunately, there is very little data that allows answering these questions.

To answer these questions, the chapter uses two approaches. This leads to the following structure: Section 2 deliberates the state of the art about BI to demonstrate that the discussions about a BI strategy and BI governance is the result of the BI development in time. Section 3 analyzes patterns in BI projects to support the activities of a BI governance and BI strategy development. Finally, a conclusion and an outlook on further research activities are done in the final Sect. 4.

2 State of the Art: Business Intelligence

This state of the art section offers an overview about the development of BI research topics since 1956. It makes obvious that the increasing amount of BI implementations and the increasing enterprise wide usage of BI leads to the need for a BI governance and therefore to a support by conceptual approaches like maturity models.

[1] It is not the chapter's goal to discuss existing design rationale for maturity models such as described in Knackstedt R, Pöppelbuß J, Becker J (2009) Vorgehensmodell zur Entwicklung von Reifegradmodellen In: Proceedings of 9th international conference on business informatics, Vienna, Austria, pp 535–544, or de Bruin T, Freeze R, Kulkarni U, Rosemann M (2005) Understanding the main phases of developing a maturity assessment model. In: Proceedings of 16th Australasian conference on information systems, Sydney, Australia.

2.1 Conceptual Approach to Business Intelligence

The amount of empirical work in BI has been substantial and diverse. A precise assignment of the term BI is challenging and there is a lack of a consistent definition in literature. Quintessence is that it is understood as a process of multidimensional analysis of crucial information. BI is influenced by a technological, an organizational, and an environmental context [12], as shown in Fig. 1. The technological context includes the internal and external technologies that are relevant to the firm. The organizational context refers to the characteristics and resources of the firm, including the firm's size, degree of centralization, degree of formalization, managerial structure, human resources, amount of slack resources, and linkages among employees. The environmental context includes size and structure of the industry, the firm's competitors, the macroeconomic context, and the regulatory environment [12].

An adoption model based on Tornatzky and Fleischer tailored for BI is proposed as basis for shaping the view onto BI. In a broad context, the model ties together factors representing three major contexts of BI developments in time: *environment*, *technology*, and *organization and BI governance*. The environmental context of the Tornatzky and Fleischer framework is relabeled as *business environment* to better reflect the business driven attributes of BI. The context *technology* follows the definition of the Tornatzky and Fleischer framework. It highlights the perceived

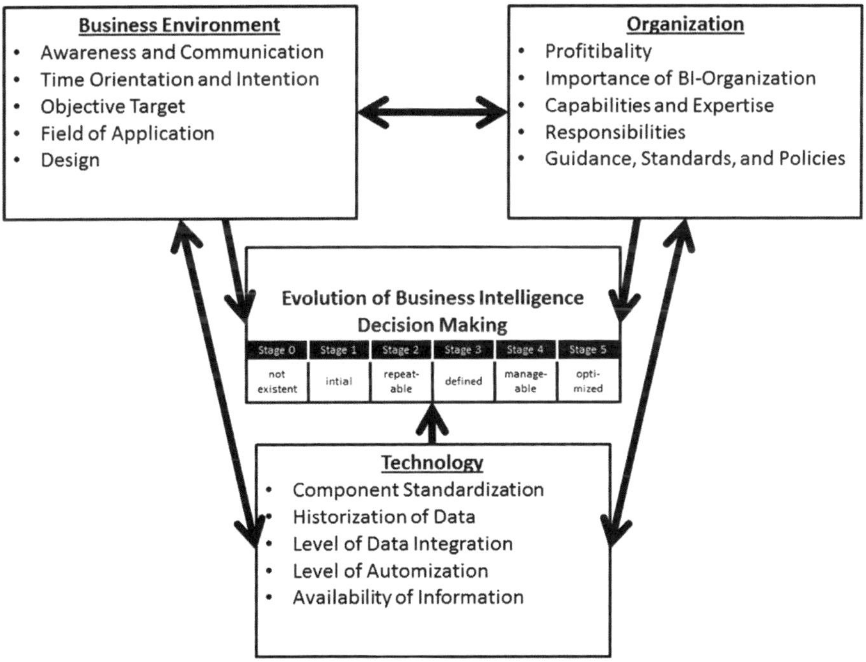

Fig. 1 Technology-organization-business environment-framework

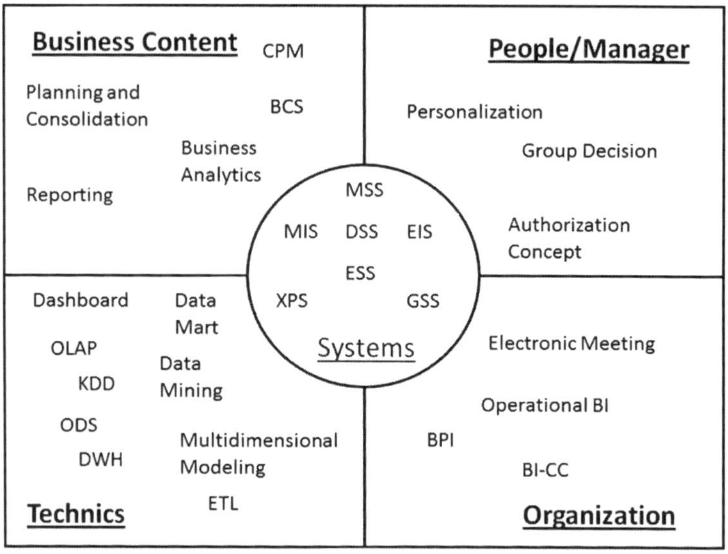

Fig. 2 Four quadrants scheme on Business Intelligence

benefits and the ability to adopt. Since BI has a direct impact on the functional IT core, the organizational context suggested by Tornatzky and Fleischer, refers to the organization and governance. It is labeled as *organization and BI governance* to reflect its focus.

The IT Performance Measurement Maturity Model of Becker et al. [1] serves as a basis, because it integrates all existing BI maturity models of Eckerson [3] and Chamoni/Gluchowski [2] with the IT-Balanced Scorecard [5], CObIT [8], and CMMI [9] to be able to identify and classify BI developments in organizations. The IT Performance Measurement Maturity Model, as stage oriented one, is put into the Technology-Organization-Environment Framework, to frame the discussion.

Figure 2 organizes discussed BI topics into the dimensions of the Technology-Organization-Business Environment Framework to show the area of conflict.

Characteristics of *Business Environment*

The *business* dimension is described by the usage of components along management processes, levels, and roles. There is evidence that intense task demands of managers stimulate the rapid diffusion of an innovation since the late 1970s [7]. When managers face a complex and rapidly changing environment, IT is both necessary and justified [10]. Market and environmental factors, such as the degree of competition or regulation in the market, the stability of demand for the products, and the degree of loyalty of the customers, cannot be controlled by the management of organizations, but can affect the way its business is conducted. From an IT viewpoint, management will demand more responsiveness and flexibility in IT support to gain an appropriate task support of the managers to fulfill their information needs.

Characteristics of *Technology*

Following the aforementioned systematization, the concepts Data Warehouse (DW) including the components ETL, Operational Data Store, Enterprise DW, Data Mart, and dashboards are assigned to the *technology* dimension. The influence of technology characteristics on the IT adoption has been studied fairly extensively [6]. An important group of factors are those related to the cost-benefit trade-off of implementing a particular technology. A quantification of the cost and benefits related to BI may lead toward perceptions of the possible gains and barriers. The first factor represents perceived benefits of adopting BI in relation to an organization's specific setting. It is advocated that BI systems provide an environment that is no longer constrained by individual/spread sheet oriented systems, promote analyzing flexibility and information integration, and allow transparent data access. These benefits are consistently perceived worldwide.

BI systems require a substantial degree of technical competence to be able to deal with automization, data integration, and fast reliable availability of information. In case of BI systems, major barriers include the system's migration, the technical expertise of existing IT staff members and the degree of entrenchment with a proprietary technology. BI systems seem to possess some common properties. First, each BI system represents a unique way to interconnect a large number of hardware and software components at least as a necessary information source. The level of complexity grows exponentially not only with the number of components, but also with the different versions of the same component like it is common in today's organizations. Second, a BI system is not an artifact that can be mass produced with identical characteristics. Third, the development and management of a BI system requires not only knowledge of individual hardware and software components, but also their interconnection arrangement as well as an updated knowledge of a large number of standards that are undergoing rapid changes themselves. The breadth and depth of knowledge required are likely to set barriers to potential implementations of BI systems.

Characteristics of *Organization*

The *organization* dimension consists of business processes, which have to be supported, and processes concerning designing, operating, and changing BI systems. Depending on the existing practices some organizations may require more efforts to introduce IT in general than others. In context of BI systems implementation three factors are proposed: complexity of the existing IT infrastructure, satisfaction level with existing systems, and degree of formalization of systems development and management.

Standard compliance as one requirement of a BI governance extends the process of standardization from technical items to related administrative procedures such as procurement and system development. Companies that currently have a formal policy on system-related matters are better prepared to adopt BI systems for at least two reasons. First, the enforcement of standard compliance requires setting up procurement and testing procedures. Organizations that already have a formal system policy in piece incur a much lower overhead to establish new policy and procedures developed for BI systems. Second, the requirements of interoperability and interconnectivity apply to all levels of an infrastructure ranging from hardware, system software and applications. A high level of formalization within the IT function implies a wider and more detailed control at each system level.

Within the fourth square of Fig. 2, *people* dimension and their respective tasks, two types of decision-making can be differentiated: group decisions or personalized decisions. In this area of conflict and with regard to the degree of support, approaches vary between highly automated ones like predictive analytics and information inquiries.

2.2 Literature Review

The literature review is an appropriate method following *Webster and Watson* [14], *Fettke* [4] as well as *vom Brocke* [13]. The chosen analysis is concept-centric. Therefore, the focus of selected publications results from an underlying context to BI. The basis is a listing of relevant sources and publications, which underlie a double-blind review process. The relevance of a journal within this literature research is correlated with the *Jourqual2* ranking. Used databases were Ebsco, Academic Source Complete (ASC), Business Source Complete (BSC), Springer Link (SL), and Science Direct (SD). The selection considers English as well as German language articles. Duplicates were finally eliminated. Contributions from reference lists of relevant articles were considered additionally. Book chapters were excluded, because of lacking double-blind reviews. The classification of identified publications was made following other systematic literary analysis and it follows the proposed Technology-Organization-Business-Environment Framework.

Altogether, 91,264 articles in 3,688 journals (1956 until 2010) have been analyzed and scored corresponding the four proposed dimensions by using a Likert scale (1 = strongly disagree/no match up to 5 = strongly agree/core topic). Each article was evaluated by a four-eye principle. In case of inconsistency, a third reviewer was consulted to evaluate the documents.

Table 1 shows that overall, all categories include a comparable amount of papers. Just people/manager is below-average. The mean of the Likert scale values indicate a slightly oscillating time series of measured BI dimensions, which are uniformly distributed over the years.

Table 1 Distribution of research papers within the defined categories

	Business	Technic	Organization	People/manager
Overall	27.00 %	26.50 %	28.50 %	18.00 %
Mean (Likert scale)	2.04	2.00	2.15	1.35

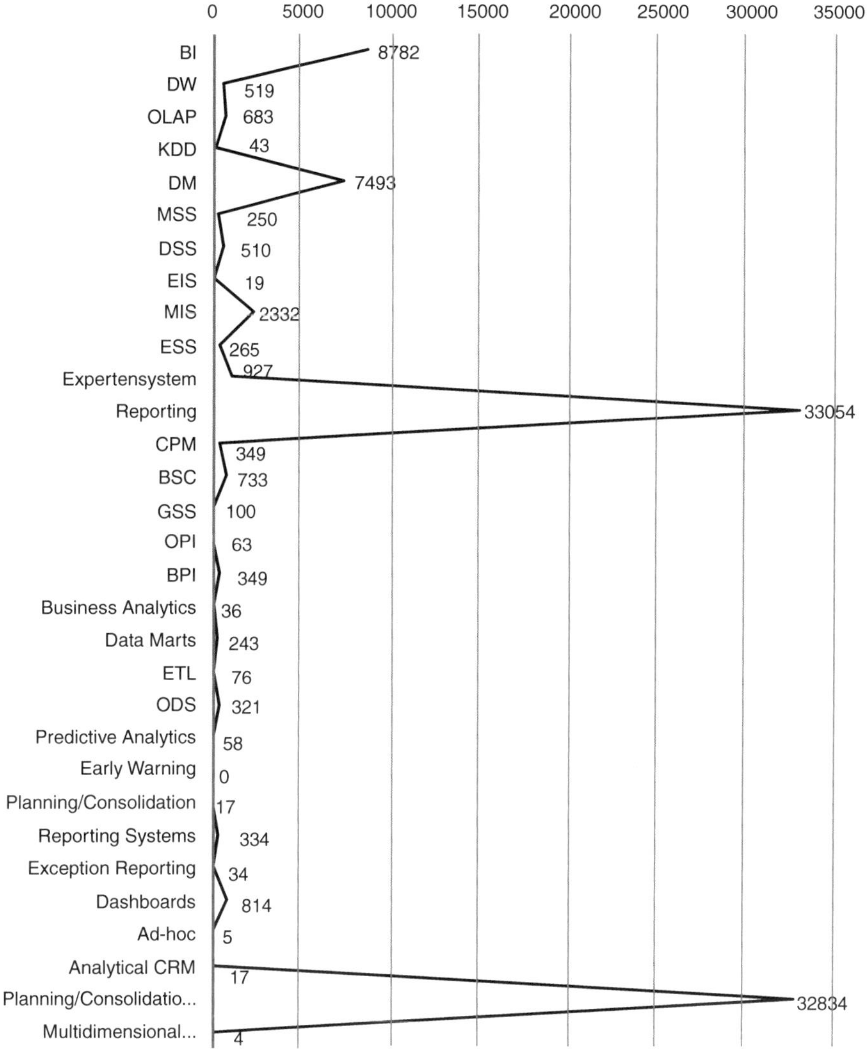

Fig. 3 Occurrence of search terms

An analysis of the amount of papers per entered search term can be regarded in Fig. 3. The data unveils *reporting*, as search term of the category business content, as dominant term. The term *Business Intelligence* emerges in the mid of the 1980s, even more pronounced in the mid of the 1990s. Little later, at the end of the 1990s, the concepts of *OLAP*, *Business Analytics,* and *ETL* appear. Most intense BI activities in companies happened in the last 15 years. The discussion about BICCs is growing in the recent years.

3 Framework to Structure Patterns in BI Projects

We used submissions of *The Data Warehousing Institute, Germany* (TDWI) best practice competition. A total of 45 projects of different companies from the years 2005–2010 were examined. This includes industry, application area, initial situation, amount of users, selected solution, used resources and leads to the following structure (Fig. 4).

Table 2 shows that the analyzed BI projects differ in all characteristics either independent from their respective industry or department or enterprise-wide coverage. The shown project evaluation structure can be enhanced with the respective project data to offer a guideline for management decisions in context of BI projects.

In order to evaluate the projects on a very first stage, the respective business fields and affected levels of the organization are analyzed. Depending on these factors the discussion is guided by the implementation and project characteristics, too.

Technology The chosen technical solutions range from Microsoft Excel integrated open source tools to all-covering software suites. All projects have in common that they are addressing all BI systems layers; starting at the ETL layer up to the data storage and data analyzing layer. The differences are based in the used software and

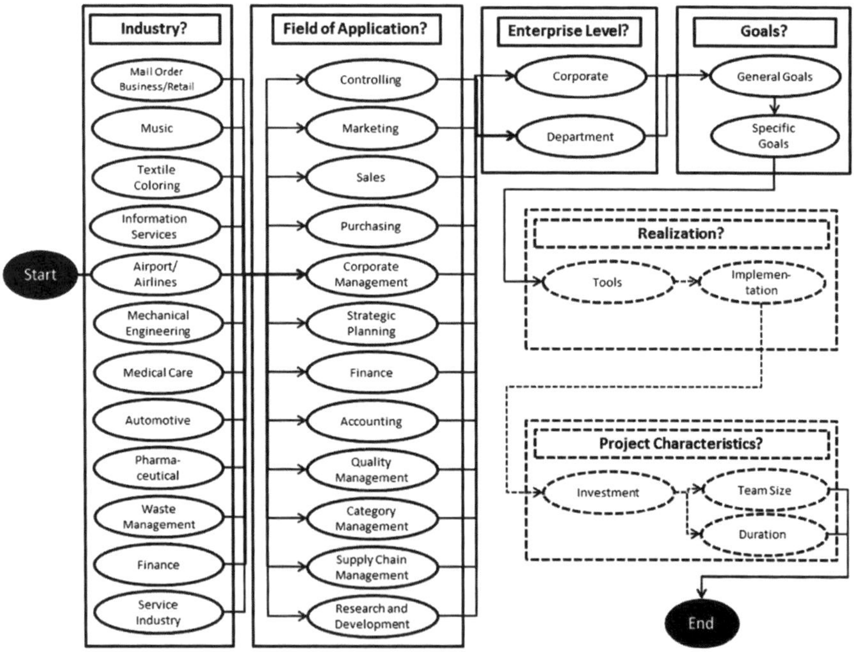

Fig. 4 BI project evaluation structure

Table 2 Statistics regarding overall data set

	Min	Max	Median	Standard deviation
User	2	1,500	259.6098	363.2249
Project duration (in month)	1.5	80	10.4634	11.9869
Project cost (in Euro)	6,200.00	9,500,000.00	878,443.82	2,027,590.72
Number of cubes	1	1,100	74	210.9838
Number of dimensions	5	1,200	76.4375	214.4148

due to this, if the software offers already prepared modules or content to gain faster project results.

Organization The projects differ in their organizational background. Some have their focus on department oriented solutions; others try to cover enterprise wide activities. But all agree to analyze the underlying processes. Due to the reason that IT departments and especially BICCs deal as service provider, all projects have in common that user satisfaction is measured. Differences are just in the realization: some do specific workshops on this topic; others are measuring the system's usage and feedback on hotlines.

Business Environment All the project descriptions match in their respective project need definition. Market or environmental factors like competition are named in all competition contributions as underlying background. Known reasons like data quality improvement or increasing transparency were not shown.

4 Conclusions

The discussion about BI maturity models is a logical result of the BI evolution. With the growing number of isolated BI projects in companies there is a lack of support in organizing these activities. Usually maturity models are chosen to give orientation for the realization of a BI strategy. Maturity models require the documentation of business processes, which often leads to more administrational effort. Only huge companies and international corporations can afford this effort, yet. Therefore a BI evaluation structure is introduced, which organizes best practice data about project planning and budgeting to be able to position the own company in relation to others.

Expert discussions have shown that this structure is suitable for a target oriented and controlled implementation of BI concepts in companies to benefit from lessons learned. The experts unanimously hold the opinion that the evaluation structure is clear, but indicates experiential concerns. Ultimately, the given reference character was discovered the evaluation structure to accelerate the implementation, in order to produce faster results in project definitions.

For future research it is necessary to analyze the project data more deeply and to develop a decision support system for a strategy based BI project planning system. As a result an ontology map will give insight into development paths.

References

1. Becker J, Knackstedt R, Pöppelbuß J, Schwarze L (2008) Das IT Performance Measurement Maturity Model—Ein Reifegradmodell für die Business Intelligence-Unterstützung des IT-Managements
2. Chamoni P, Gluchowski P (2004) Integrationstrends bei Business-Intelligence-Systemen. Wirtschaftsinformatik 46(2):119–128
3. Eckerson W (2006) Performance dashboards: measuring, monitoring, and managing your business. Wiley, Hoboken, NJ
4. Fettke P (2006) State-of-the-Art des State-of-the-Art—Eine Untersuchung der Forschungsmethode "Review" innerhalb der Wirtschaftsinformatik. Wirtschaftsinformatik 48(4):257–266
5. Grembergen W, Saull R (2001) Aligning business and information technology through the balanced scorecard at a major Canadian financial group. Its status measured with an IT BSC maturity model. In: Proceedings of the 34th international conference on system sciences, Hawaii
6. Kwon TH, Zmud RW (1987) Unifying the fragmented models of information systems implementation. In: Boland JR, Hirschheim R (eds) Critical issues in information systems research. Wiley, New York, pp 227–251
7. Mansfield E, Rapoport J, Romeo A, Villani E, Wagner S, Husic F (1977) The production and application of new industrial technology. Norton, New York
8. n. A. IT Governance Institute: CobiT 4.0!. The IT Governance Institute
9. n. A. (2006) CMMI for development. http://www.sei.cmu.edu/pub/documents/06.reports/pdf/06tr008.pdf. Accessed 24 June 2010
10. Pfeffer J, Leblebici H (1977) Information technology and organizational structure. Pac Sociol Rev 20(2):241–261
11. Schulze K-D, Besbak U, Dinter B (2009) Business Intelligence Studie. Steria Mummert, Hamburg
12. Tornatzky LG, Fleischer M (1990) The processes of technological innovation. Lexington Books, Lexington, MA
13. vom Brocke J, Simons A, Niehaves B, Riemer K, Plattfaut R, Cleven A (2009) Reconstructing the giant: on the importance of rigour in documenting the literature search process. In: Newell S, Whitley E, Pouloudi N, Wareham J, Mathiassen L (eds) Proceedings of the 17th European conference on information systems, Verona, Italy, pp 2206–2217
14. Webster J, Watson RT (2002) Analyzing the past to prepare for the future: writing a literature review. MIS Q 26(2):xiii–xxiii

Deployment of a Descriptive Big Data Model

Marco Pospiech and Carsten Felden

Abstract Big Data is an emerging research topic. The term remains fuzzy and jeopardizes to become an umbrella term. Straight forward investigations are inhibited since the research field is not well defined, yet. To identify a common understanding, experts have been interviewed. Hereby, the findings are coded and conceptualized until a descriptive Big Data model is developed by using Grounded Theory. This provides the basis for the model's deployment. Here, academic publications and practical implementations marked as Big Data are classified. It becomes evident that Big Data is use-case driven and forms an interdisciplinary research field. Even not all papers belong to this research field. The findings become confirmed by the practical implementations. The chapter contributes to the intensive discussion about the term Big Data in illustrating the underlying area of discourse. A classification to set the research area apart from others can be achieved to support a goal oriented research in future.

Keywords Big Data • Grounded theory • Interview • Qualitative research

1 Introduction

The amount of various business data is growing exponential while their accompanied storing and processing in a traditional way makes a task fulfillment complicated. In this context, the term Big Data occurs increasingly in scientific discussions and publications [1]. A common definition belongs to Gartner: "*Big data* is high-volume, high-velocity, and high-variety information assets that demand cost-effective innovative forms of information processing for enhanced insight and decision making" [2], but considering others, existing definitions are diverse. For example, Bizer et al. [3] follow a semantic perspective and whereby others focusing on processing huge amounts of data [4]. As a consequence, two major issues are conspicuous. On the one hand side, the positioning of goal oriented publications to solve business administration related problems within a Big Data context is

M. Pospiech (✉) • C. Felden
Technische Universität Bergakademie, Freiberg, Germany
e-mail: marco.pospiech@bwl.tu-freiberg.de; carsten.felden@bwl.tu-freiberg.de

J.H. Mayer, R. Quick (eds.), *Business Intelligence for New-Generation Managers*,
DOI 10.1007/978-3-319-15696-5_7

impeded [1]. On the other hand side, already established research areas such as High Performance Computing (HPC) tend to recoin themselves as Big Data to obtain more attention [5]. Thus, the possible research field of Big Data is fuzzy and the term seems to be only used as marketing buzzword. So, the demand of a theoretical base has already been stated since relevant topics and related theories are unknown [1]. In this context, the work isolates the inherent nature of the Big Data topic and to deduce a descriptive model as first step. It is the chapter 's goal, to illustrate the applicability and deployment for practice and research. Thus, research areas are stronger defined to set Big Data apart from and business administrated issues can be addressed.

A quantitative proof of the fuzzy term Big Data seems to be not possible since underlying factors are unknown. In addition, no research has been published, yet, which addresses a theoretical reprocessing of this topic. It is helpful that already Miles and Huberman [6] indicate that qualitative methods are useful in an early state of research to gain a professional perspective based on longstanding experience. In this context, we accomplished expert interviews to gain the consent understanding [7]. Results are coded and conceptualized by using Grounded Theory [8, 9]. A Big Data description model is derived that represents expert opinions. The resulting categories can be used as patterns for future Big Data research and practical implementations to define the research area apart from others. Hereby, the chapter contributes to the intensive discussion about the term Big Data in illustrating the underlying area of discourse.

The papers's concourse is as follows: Sect. 2 provides the research design. Hereby, expert interviews and Grounded Theory as method are briefly shown to be able to create an appropriate basis. The proceeding of methods is illustrated, thus, a rigor research design can be ensured. Section 3 provides the descriptive model. Single categorizes are presented and discussed. The model is used in Sect. 4. Hereby, several Big Data papers and implementations are classified whether they belong to Big Data or not. So the model application and its term specification of Big Data get evident. The chapter is summarized in Sect. 5, where implications and further research topics are highlighted.

2 Research Design

The research design is subdivided into four stages (see Fig. 1). After stating the research goal and problem formulation, we conduct a literature review [10] in a second step to arrange the existing knowledge about Big Data models. Academic databases like *IEEE xplore*, *AIS library*, *ScienceDirect*, and *EBSCOhost Web* were used and relevant papers were identified through the search items *Big Data Theory* and *Big Data Model* in keywords, title, and abstract. In fact, no article was identified. Thus, no published research exists that addresses a specification of the term Big Data through a theoretical approach. Due to this reason, we decided to use expert interviews to obtain initial insights. Expert interviews are based on different phases.

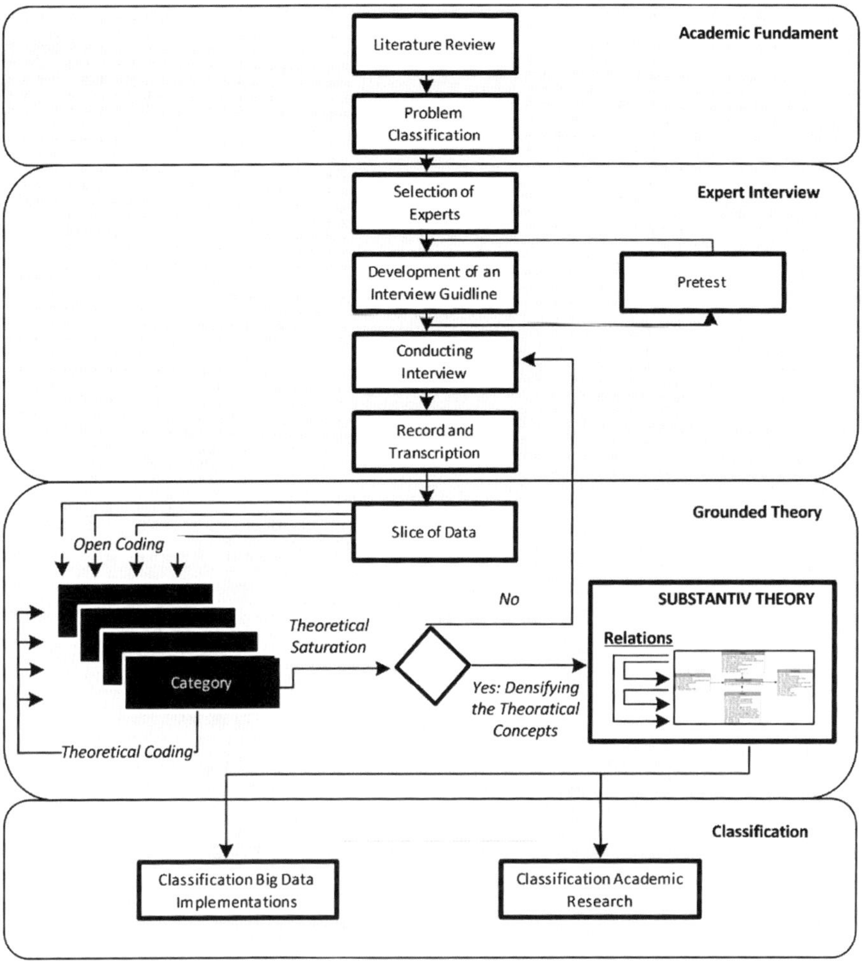

Fig. 1 Research design (Based on [8, 9])

They address the problem and eligible experts as well as a guideline based interview conducting and evaluation [7]. Within the execution, 20 experts from international acting IT companies were interviewed. To ensure the expert's competence, a minimum of 1 year Big Data experience was assumed.

The telephone interviews varied between 30 and 60 min and were conducted between July and December 2012. Comparability of the results is ensured through interview guidelines. Thereby, pretests were conducted. As a result, characteristics, key drivers, definitions, distinctions, potentials, use-cases, issues, strategies of Big Data, and expert statistics were gathered. All interviews were recorded and transcribed.

Grounded Theory [8] collects and analyzes qualitative data (like expert interviews) and is accepted and widespread in information systems research [11].

The method aims the generation of conceptual properties, categories, and relationships through a combination of inductive, deductive, and abductive reasoning in iterative cycles. The usage in an early research status to describe a phenomenon is often applied [12]. Big Data belongs to a relative new research area without existing theoretical fundament, yet. Thus, Grounded Theory is used here since the generation and discovering of concepts and inherent relationships relies to the strengths of the method [9].

The analysis in Grounded Theory consists of four steps [9]. Within the open coding, so called *slices of data* (transcribed interviews) are broken down into several categories. These categories are described in terms of their properties. Thereby, several categories were assigned to the transcribed interview passages, thus similar statements get apparent. This is followed by the theoretical coding, where relations between categories are established. Thereby, new *slices of data* are added and categorized until a theoretical saturation arises and no novel category emerges. Three researches were involved during the model development until all agreed in a theoretical saturation. The result is a substantive approach, which is applicable to the emerging particular area. It is recommended to use existing coding schemata within the theoretical coding, because the negation of them leads usually to confused and unclear theoretically coding [9]. An often used one belongs to [13], where the phenomenon (Big Data) belongs to the center. The original reasons of emergence, the context, possible strategies to face the phenomenon, and consequences are put into relation. To allow a common understanding, Strauss and Corbin [13] defined the categories as follows:

- Phenomenon: The central idea, event, happening, incident about which a set of actions or interactions are directed at managing, handling, or to which the set of actions is related.
- Causal Conditions: The term refers to the events or incidents that lead to the occurrence or development of a phenomenon. Also look at its specific properties and dimensions, which in fact should be explainable by looking back at the specific dimensions of the causal conditions.
- Context: Represents the particular set of conditions within which the action/ interactional strategies are taken to manage, handle, carry out, and respond to a specific phenomenon.
- Strategy: Action devised to manage, handle, carry out, and respond to a phenomenon under a specific set of perceived conditions and context. Actions have certain properties. First, it is processual, evolving in nature. Thus it can be studied in terms of sequences, or in term of movement, or change over time. Second, action/interaction is purposeful, goal oriented, done for some reason—in response to or to manage a phenomenon.
- Consequences: Outcomes or results of action and interaction. Consequences may be actual or potential, happen in the present or in the future.

As a result, all identified categories were shrunken until a substantive model emerged. Exemplary scientific Big Data publications and practical implementations marked as Big Data are classified to illustrate how the model supports the academic and practical sharpening of the term.

3 Descriptive Model

The five categories being used and their subcategories are described in this chapter and discussed. Numbers in brackets belongs to the amount of experts stating a category. E.g., (10/20) mean out of 20 probates, 10 mentioned this category. Thus, the importance of a component is illustrated. This supports the verification whether a Big Data paper belongs to the research area.

3.1 Phenomenon

In general, Big Data can be seen as such a *phenomenon* described above and emerges through *context* and *causal conditions*. This gets apparent since popular terms volume, velocity, and variety [2] are implied. This leads to the point that Big Data can be understood as circumstance, in which an increased data volume must be processed or/and stored. In fact, *strategies* to face this *phenomenon* will change in time. But they can always be subdivided into a functional and technology part. The *consequences* are resulting from all schema categories and are issue and advantage related. Considering this proposed approach, all mentioned categories are not novel. They are representing own and nowadays mostly well researched disciplines, which emerged by their own causal conditions and context. Based on gained experiences and use-cases of this single disciplines in past emerged the *phenomenon* Big Data. It applies that a combination of the underlying disciplines achieves a higher value as a single discipline can obtain for its own. The combination of these concepts will only be useful, if a specific idea exists, which produces a positive value. Since the underlying disciplines are data-intensive the *phenomenon* Big Data is into place. In this context, Big Data represents an interdisciplinary research area and is use-case driven. Figure 2 shows the describing Big Data model.

3.2 Causal Condition

In fact, most *causal conditions* are well-known and defining Big Data not by itself. The requirements can be summarized as a need for an extensive environmental understanding. Experts stated a particular demand on monitoring, prediction, and decision support as well as a need to explain circumstances in natural sciences. New possibilities are seen through *context* and *strategy*, which enable the achievement of an improved understanding as before. In a dynamic world, this knowledge must be

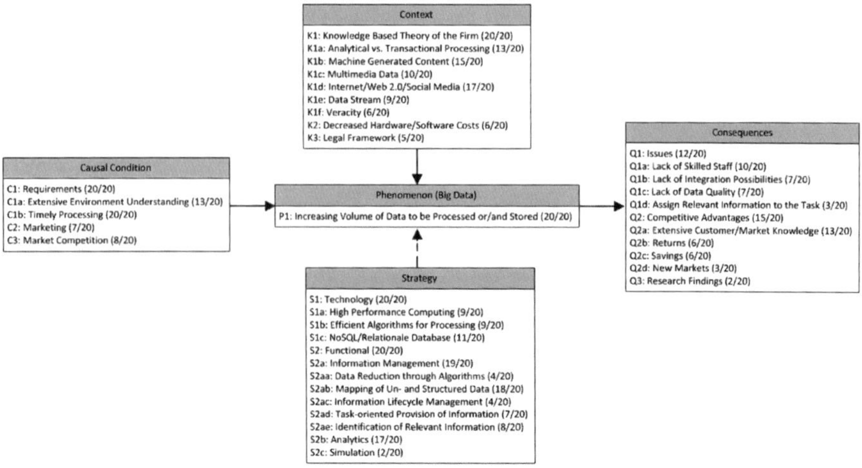

Fig. 2 Big Data descriptive model

increasingly produced in a timely manner [14]. Hereby, time adequate processing belongs as one part to velocity [2]. Concepts like decision latency or automatization [15] represent core aspects and are often mentioned. Hence, information technology tasks must accomplish user needs in time. Besides requirements are two more causes.

One often applied aspect belongs to marketing. Hereby, experts stated the possibility that Big Data is not novel and only driven by sales persons to maximum their revenue. In this case, Big Data is no new research area and should be ignored by academics. Comparable statements can be found for Business Intelligence (BI), which counts today as one of the most important fields for practice and academic in information systems [16]. This leads to the point that further work has to proof, whether Big Data is solely marketing driven or not.

Another causal condition belongs to market competition and is therefore a drivig force which is known in lots of technology related projects, e.g. Customer Relationship Management (CRM) or Efficient Consumer Response (ECR). It is slightly related to the requirements since it represents the source of them. In dynamic markets, companies have to reduce production cycles, safe costs, identify early trends, react fast, and maximize their profit in a sustainable way. Similar causal conditions can be found for BI in Gluchowski et al. In past, BI was mostly driven by the need of a timely processing and an extended environment understanding to survive in a competitive market. Even a discussion whether BI belongs to a buzzword can be obtained [14]. Thus, the *causal conditions* are common, alone. A more unique Big Data field emerges trough the combination of *context* and *causal conditions*.

3.3 Context

Context describes the circumstances in which Big Data evolved. During our coding, we recognized that most of all context related expert statements were already shown the Knowledge Based Theory (KBT) of the Firm [17]. Here, experts stated: "For the purpose of decision support, different data sources and structures must be consolidated to achieve a most extensive acquisition of information" or "Formats, structures and sources must be integrated to acquire competitive advantages" or "The novelty of Big Data consists besides huge data volume within the usage of heterogeneous sources and formats". In this work, KPT is rather used as concept as a theory and should not interpreted as a mapping mechanism to Grounded Theory. Thus, the KBT of the Firm considers knowledge as unique and most strategically significant resource [17] by focusing on knowledge integration and combination to achieve a competitive advantage [18]. According to [19] information technologies are able to support firms within the KBT since it can be used to synthesize, enhance, and expedite large-scale intra- and inter-firm knowledge management. In this context, an increasing trend is noticeable that integrates various data sources, structures and formats to obtain a competitive advantage. On a practical view, this is also known as variety [2].

However, the KBT arises also through underlying reasons. An expert stated an increasing awareness of analyzing transaction data. Hereby, transactions are no longer the fundamental basis of analyses as we understand it in BI [14] but rather an explanatory variable. Hereby, the way why a transaction appears (e.g. interaction data analysis of Social Media, forum, web shop, GPS tracking, etc. of a customer until the purchase) comes more and more into focus to gain a more extensive environment view.

Another subcategory is seen in machine generated content. It relies to any data consisting discrete events that have been created automatically from a computer application, process or other machines in absents of any human intervention [21]. In this context, experts stated the increasing IT pervasion. Thus, research and practice find themselves in a world of radio-frequency identification (RFID) chips, log files, internet of thinks, GPS tracking (vehicles and mobile phones), and any kind of sensor technology that can be used to gain an extensive environment understanding. In most of the cases, this type of data occurs as stream.

In streaming, a continuous flow of data must be handled. This data relies often to semi-structured time series and implies issues of storing and processing since the permanent transfer produces an enormous data volume. In contrast to static data, only a subset of data can be considered [22]. Experts stated that in most of the cases streaming data must be analyzed in real time. In addition, science application produces stream data where the storing of all features is not possible.

Other key drivers are seen in Internet, Web 2.0, and Social Media. Most of the Big Data *phenomena* occur through the Internet. One aspect belongs to the physical infrastructure, which enables a world spanning interconnection through all participants and consequently an exchange of information and data. Only through this infrastructure, the realization of concepts like cloud, grid, or distributed computing got possible. In addition, it acts as immense information storage for every participant. Besides that, experts stated the fact that the internet evolved as interactive platform where people collaborate and share information, also known as Web 2.0 [23]. Within this movement companies like Google, Yahoo!, Twitter, eBay, Amazon, or Facebook emerged. The rapidly growing content and users forced the companies to develop cost effective and scalable technologies. Here, technologies like MapReduce or Hadoop emerged and are now patterns for further applications [24]. Besides that, Web 2.0 enabled the extensive creation and exchange of various user generated content. User generated content belongs to contributed data, information or media not created by the provider of the web service itself. Examples are hotel ratings, wikis, or videos. This kind of information has rapidly grown during the last years and provides an interesting analysis fundament [20]. One of the most important applications of Web 2.0 belongs to the Social Media [25]. In this context, most of the experts stated that the step into Social Media enables the most exciting possibility to gain a more advanced view about customer and environment as before.

Another aspect belongs to the data type itself. While in past, only structured data went into the analyzed focus, possibilities raised to interpret and gain information automatically from multimedia sources nowadays (image, video, audio, and text). Thus, human generated content gets machine-readable. Prominent examples are seen in text mining or video and image sentiment analysis.

This new types of data and sources implicate another *context*. Whereby traditional data was clean and precise the new ones are rather fuzzy. Text mining or sentiment analyses are always a translation from human content to machine-readable data. During this procedure, information gets lost and diffuse. Even a tracking system with data from vehicle and mobile devices does not work precisely. In addition, combining unknown sources means also unknown data quality. This aspect is already known as veracity [26], but applications have to deal with these uncertainties.

The increasing improvements in storage and processing technologies are also stated as one reason for Big Data. Especially, associated cost savings enables the implementation of scalable systems. Thus, companies and research organizations can fulfill their requirements within the budget limitation. Another aspect belongs to the open source movement. Thus, the generation of content within the internet remains in most of the cases free of cost. In addition, key Big Data technologies are usually open source tools. Here, organizations observing saving possibilities through projects like Hadoop or MangoDB.

In addition, the legal framework represents a relevant *context*. Experts stated that besides all possibilities of Big Data most of all future applications are situated between data privacy restrictions. Thus, it is not legal to combine different sources to gain a broader view over customer and environment, always. Legislation depends on the country and must be proofed in detail. Furthermore, users are developing awareness of data privacy. As a result, countries have to define a framework where users rights are guaranteed and new Big Data concepts are enabled.

3.4 Strategy

As already stated, the inherent nature of Big Data is not defined by *strategy* (shown as punctuate arrow). *Strategy* is necessary to overcome the *phenomenon* but is not an essential component. Hereby, *strategy* is stretched through technology and functional aspects. Technology addresses the *phenomenon* (caused by *context* and *causal conditions*) and is not limited in future. Experts agree in three concepts.

HPC belongs to intensive calculation or storing tasks. The processing of those jobs through personal computer is not appropriate. Thus, concepts like cloud, grid, distributed, and parallel computing are implied and mentioned. The nature of these concepts allows the scaling of needed hardware to fulfill the task in an appropriate manner [27].

Besides high performance hardware, efficient working algorithms were also mentioned. Thus, the time and computation complexity of traditional algorithms suffers. All steps of processing, storing, and analyzing are time relevant in Big Data and need to be supported. One possible solution refers to [28]. In addition, parallel programming models took place into Big Data technologies. Here, Googles MapReduce was often mentioned, where the framework specifies map and reduce functions to execute them in a parallel way [29].

An important part of technologies belongs to the database discussion. Some experts argue relational databases are not able to meet the requirements due the lack of scalability and query performance, where others allude proceedings in relational databases. Often stated NoSQL approaches are key-value, column, or document oriented databases. Besides the discussion between NoSQL and relational databases, the movement to in-memory technologies was also often mentioned. Nevertheless, this kind of technologies enables the computation and storing of high volume data in a proper time. The processing of heterogeneous data sources cannot be solved by just technology.

Thus, the second *strategy* belongs to functional concept. Expert believes that the Big Data *phenomenon* can be tackled through organizational approaches. Hereby, information management (IM) is mentioned. IM aims the efficient utilization of information in respect of the organizational goal. It manages information systems, overarching executive functions and information and communication technologies as well as the handling of information in an economic way. The last one belongs to information logistic, information lifecycle, information demand, information source, information quality, information provision and usages management [30]. During the interviews experts stated several Big Data related aspects to the information management. Hereby, already common approaches like BI were mentioned. But, not all concepts are transferable to Big Data. In future, existing methods must be proofed of Big Data suitability. If not, new methods will emerge.

One core concept belongs to the mapping of structured and unstructured (image, text, audio, video) data. In this context, Big Data application designers must combine various data sources in a useful manner to gain a broader view about reality. Nevertheless, available concepts are rare to guide those activities [1]. Industry experts have to figure out what kind of data sources can support the target activity. In addition, semantic concepts are seen as possible benefit within the combination of various sources.

Another aspect is seen in the task-oriented provision of information. This aspect shares similar aspects to information logistic. Both address the provision of the right information, at the right time, in the right amount and place in an adequate quality. Thereby, information logistics consider only the data flow. The flow of unstructured data is often uncertain. In addition, information logistic neglects the value of information itself [30].

Information lifecycle management is also seen as one possible aspect within Big Data *strategies*. It aims the creation of an equal status between information demand and supply. Hereby, an update of both in an iterative cycle is necessary. Especially within Big Data information management is important, because various data sources and information technology are used whereby quality has to be ensured. Besides that, storage aspects have to be considered. Thus, most of the information loses value in time and a continuous storing remains questionable.

The identification of relevant information can support this aspect. This can be done through management methods as well as through machine learning based techniques. Experts stated that task relevant information must be automatically declared within data sources. This is essential, especially in Big Data.

Another field belongs to the data reduction. As in information identification this can be done through management or mathematical methods. Thereby, any kind of technique that allows a more efficient way of handling data without losing relevant information has to be considered. Possible works can be seen in [31].

17 of 20 experts labeled the analyses of Big Data as core concept. Through the stated *context* and *causal condition* several kinds of analysis techniques evolved and are now considered in Big Data. The most mentioned method belongs to the Knowledge Discovery in Database (KDD) also referred to as Data Mining. It represents the non-trivial process of identifying valid, novel, potentially useful, and ultimately understandable patterns in data [32]. There exist several mentioned subcategories of Data Mining. Text Mining transfers unstructured textual data into a machine-readable content, which is subsequently used by machine based learning techniques [33]. Another one belongs to Web Mining. This can be categorized into content, structure, and usage mining [34]. Similar approaches were stated for image, audio and video analyzes. A typical example can be seen by [35]. Even the growing Social Media brings new practices along. One often stated example is seen in social network analyses, where pattern of relationships and interactions between social actors are analyzed to discover underlying structures [36]. Predictive Analytics was often mentioned, which addresses the predictions of the future itself [37]. Certain participants remarked that the nature of Big Data prevents modeling and cleansing. Here, the data must be processed on-the-fly. Another analyses focus

is seen within the detection of relationships between different data sources. Thus, analysts are supported in hypothesizing. Besides the stated analyze concepts, experts highlighted the advanced analysis character of Big Data. Classical Online Analytical Processing (OLAP) cubes as known from BI are not included. Few experts stated the application of advanced visualization techniques. Possible examples of high volume presentation can be obtained from [38].

The final strategy belongs to simulation. Just some experts quoted this fact since it is more seen from an academic perspective. Nevertheless, in most of the cases, simulations handle voluminous data of various inputs [16]. Hereby, the processing time must be acceptable. It is defined as process, which drives a system model with suitable inputs an observing the resultant outputs, whereby simulation one process by another [39]. Examples for Big Data aided work is stated in [40].

3.5 Consequences

According to [13], a *phenomenon* always causes *consequences*. In context of Big Data, they are divided into issues, competitive advantages and research findings. The most stated problem belongs to missing Big Data experts, both technicians as well as functional oriented people. Thus, only a handful of specialists are experienced in new technologies like Hadoop or MapReduce, whereby the demand is huge. Here, universities must adjust their study programs [41]. The requirements on functional experts are enormous. Experts stated that more analytical and domain specific knowledge is necessary as well as an understanding for underlying technical processes to be able to deal with this phenomenon. Especially the functional integration of various data sources is seen as complex, but a technical integration is critical. Within the *phenomenon* data is stored in divers NoSQL approaches, most of the time schema-less. Hereby, the integration of traditional concepts remains difficult. This is aggravated by the fact data is received as stream and processed on-the-fly.

Considering veracity, a huge data quality issue arises. This affects the quality of analytical and simulation results since the kind of data remains fuzzy. Other experts stated quality regarded problems, because data sources are often obtained from third parties. Last but not least, NoSQL is mostly inconsistent.

Another issue is seen in assigning relevant information to the task. Thereby, the spectrum of possible Big Data sources is broad and not any content achieves an advanced understanding of the environment. Hence, functional experts must be supported by organisational as well as by technical methods in order to discovery valuable relationships and items within data sources. So investigations can be performed in a goal oriented way.

The second *consequence* belongs to the competitive advantages. There are closely related to the discussed *causal condition*. Thus, the most important fact is seen in gaining an extensive view about customer and market. Hereby, functional experts are supported through analytics and simulations as well as through organisational methods. Driven by the illustrated *context,* the expectation of new business ideas and markets emerged. Here, experts imagine the combination of various strategies since research enable it at the moment. In addition, the achievement of unsuccessful ambitious aims was also stated. At least, Big Data is not seen as end in itself. Financial advantages must appear. Savings can be obtained by the usage of open source, saved memory, and computational capacity as well as through an increased automatization. Depending on the analytical/simulation focus savings and returns are possible to achieve. This goes along with the KBF theory. Both, users as well as consultants stated this fact.

The final *consequence* addresses the academic application affected by Big Data. Thus, the context and current available strategies allows the exploration of new knowledge. New relationships and insights, especially within natural science, were quoted. Efficient algorithms, simulations, and analytics are highlighted to gain a broader view about the framing environment. Due to the reason that the expert's common background is business, only two experts stated these concepts.

4 Classification of Academic Publications and Implementations

We developed a descriptive model to discover Big Data's inherent nature. The research area of Big Data is interdisciplinary and belongs to the need of storing and processing a huge amount of data, driven by *context* and *causal conditions*. Around the emerging phenomenon various research disciplines has been positioned. Thus, Big Data belongs to applied sciences. Progress in the undergraduate sciences is welcome, but not part of the research field of Big Data itself, e.g. text mining, HPC, etc. To demonstrate the academic model application, we have chosen several papers out of a Big Data state-of-the-art publication randomly [1] and have classified them whether they belong to Big Data or not. The results are illustrated in Table 1. Numbers within the tables are related to the concept abbreviations in Fig. 2. State-of-the-art papers are excluded due to their informing character. Since not each single concept must be fulfilled to be Big Data, we left place for a small discussion part, which should be considered in any further model application. The amount of mentioned times enables a statement how strong the field is related to Big Data.

As illustrated in Table 1, the first three publications belong to Big Data. Hereby most of the concepts are fulfilled. In addition, not all papers [1] are Big Data. The fourth [45] remains to an application and typical strategies like MapReduce were used, but a combination of various data sources is neglected. Thus, the paper is more related to HPC. Furthermore [46], is not focused on a use-case. So the paper supports Big Data research, but relies not on the research area itself.

Similar to Table 1, five practical implementations marked as Big Data are compared and classified in Table 2. The cases are obtained from the leading association for the U.S. technology industry, TechAmerica. Among other aspects,

Table 1 Big Data descriptive model academic classification

Source	Causal condition	Context	Phenomenon	Strategy	Consequence	Big Data	Discussion
[42]	C1; C1a; C1b;	K1; K1c; K1d; K1e; K1f, K2	P1	S1; S1a: S1b; S1c; S2 S2a; S2aa; S2ab; S2b	Q1; Q1c; Q2 Q2c; Q3	Yes	The paper presents a pluggable prototype system to analyze and integrate high volume biometric data (fingerprints, iris image, facial image, voice, DNA) in real time. The system is cloud based underlying systems are HBase and ZooKeeper. Various analyses and deduplication occurs
[43]	C1a; C1b	K1; K1b; K1c; K1d; K1f	P1	S2; S2ae; S2ab; S2b; S2c	Q2; Q2a; Q2b	Yes	Web forum discussions are used to predict stock returns. Here structured data like market return, volatility, or trading volume are combined with unstructured text. Using stepwise regression and sentiment analysis
[44]	C1; C1a; C1b	K1; K1d; K1e; K1f	P1	S2; S2ab; S2b	Q1; Q1c; Q3	Yes	Enormous amount of behavioral data is explored to identify spatiotemporal dynamics of criminal events with the hope of identifying patterns in their aggregation that may be useful to predict and prevent future crimes. Hereby, relationships in both space and time, cross- and auto-correlation measures are combined
[45]	C1; C1a; C1b	K1; K1d; K2		S1: S1a; S1b; S2; S2b	Q2; Q2a; Q2b	No	The article designs a MapReduce based computing model for an option price prediction. Only price data was used as input. The combination of various data sources took no place. Thus, no Big Data publications
[46]	C1; C1b	K1; K1d; K2		S1; S1c		No	The paper proposes the use of single level data stores. Thereby, consistent and durable data structures, that on current hardware, allow programmers to safely exploit the low-latency and non-volatile aspects of new memory technologies are introduced. No application is illustrated only view concepts are fulfilled

Table 2 Big Data descriptive model implementation classification

Implementation	Causal condition	Context	Phenomenon	Strategy	Consequence	Big Data	Discussion
NARA's electronic records archive (ERA)	C1; C1b	K1; K1c; K3		S1; S1c; S2; S2a; S2ad; S2ae	Q1; Q1c; Q1d	No	ERA is designed to archive a variety of records of the U.S. government and worldwide archives. In January 2012, ERA manages about 142 TB of information representing over 7 billion objects (e-mails, images, records, aso.). Several archival and search functions were implemented. The main focus refers rather to store than to process Big Data. No analytical functions are realized. A mapping between un- and structured data does not occur
Wind energy turbine placement & maintenance	C1; C1a; C1b; C3	K1; K1b; K1c; K1e; K1f	P1	S1; S1a; S1b; S1c; S2; S2a; S2aa; S2ab; S2ad; S2ae; S2b; S2c	Q1; Q1c; Q1d; Q2; Q2a; Q2b; Q2c; Q2d; Q3	Yes	Vestas installs an average of one wind turbine every 3 h. Producing wind energy depends greatly on the placement of the turbine. Vestas established a wind placement library, which incorporates data from global weather systems with data collected from existing wind turbines, satellite images, and geographical information, more than 178 parameters in total. Analysis and simulation functions for turbine placement and power production were implemented

TerraEchos perimeter intrusion detection	C1; C1a; C1b	K1; K1a; K1c; K1e; K1f	P1	S1; S1a; S1b; S2; S2aa; S2ab; S2ad; S2b;	Q1; Q1c; Q1d; Q2	Yes	TerraEchos helps organizations protect and monitor critical infrastructure and secure borders. Distinguishing the sound of a whisper from the wind from miles away is a big challenge in order to identify potential risks. The solution continuously consumes and analyzes massive amounts of information-in-motion through HPC. In addition, the system gathers and analyzes information in real-time, maps acoustics and video data
NASA's Human spaceflight imagery collection	C1; C1a	K1; K1c		S2; S2a; S2ac	Q1; Q1b; Q1c; Q3	No	The IRD is responsible for managing a large, complex heterogeneous cyber infrastructure and one of the world's largest imagery archives and provides industry and public with the most historic human spaceflight imagery. The NASA imagery were catalogued and archived in structured and unstructured format. In addition, information lifecycle management was introduced. The main focus refers rather to storing than to processing Big Data. No analytical capabilities were implemented. A mapping between un- and structured data does not occur

(continued)

Table 2 (continued)

Implementation	Causal condition	Context	Phenomenon	Strategy	Consequence	Big Data	Discussion
National weather service (NWS)	C1; C1a; C1b	K1; K1a; K1b; K1c; K1e; K1f; K2	P1	S1; S1a; S1b; S1c; S2; S2a; S2aa; S2ab; S2ac; S2ad; S2ae; S2b; S2c	Q1; Q1c; Q3	Yes	The NWS provides weather, water, and climate data, forecast analyses and real-time warning for the protection of life and property and enhancement of the national economy. Data from satellites, ships, aircrafts, buoys and other sensors are considered. It is used as input for millions of operational models in HPC environments

the foundation analyzes the size and scope of technologies industry-impact on the economy. Thereby, more than 1.200 companies are represented by this organization including SAP, Cisco, Motorola, Apple, SAS and Amazon [47]. Three of five implementations belong to Big Data. Most of the categories are consistent with the findings. In our view, two of the implementations represent archiving cases and are not Big Data. Here, solely the data's volume is seen as major characteristic. Neither a mapping between structured and un-structured data occurs nor a timely processing. Surprisingly, most of the cases did not consider social media and technologies like Hadoop. Information management was always part of the implementation.

5 Conclusion

The chapter addressed the stated issue of a missing descriptive fundament of Big Data to prevent the establishment of a new buzzword. Hereby, expert interviews were conducted, transcribed and used as basis for a Grounded Theory design to obtain the inherent nature. Hereby, emerging concepts where categorized into *causal condition, context, phenomenon, strategy* and *consequences* until a theoretical saturation was achieved. As a result, Big Data is interdisciplinary, *context* and *causal conditions* driven and belongs to applied sciences. The usefulness of the resulting Big Data model was exemplarily tested. In this context, state-of the-art papers [1] and implementations were classified into the model and tested, whether they belong to Big Data or not. In fact, not all of them belong to this topic. Surprisingly, common topics like Hadoop or Social Media are not always part of Big Data implementations.

The resulting model contributes to the specification and classification of Big Data contents. Thus, the area of discourse is illustrated and the positioning of goal oriented publications to solve business administration related issues is assisted. So, Big Data is delimitated from existing research fields such as HPC. Hereby, the insights justify a stronger positioning of Big Data as own research field to motivate further research. Nevertheless, there are limitations. In fact, the descriptive model was an initial step to contribute to the existing discussion and offering a possible consensus about Big Data. Based on the proposed model, a quantitative analysis will follow to clarify if all categories and relationships are significant. In this context, it has to be proven, whether Big Data is marketing driven or not. Another gap arises through the expert selection. Thus, only IT companies were considered. In fact, besides business Big Data applications are also stated in science [10]. In this context, academics must be interviewed as well to gain the opportunity that new concepts might appear.

References

1. Pospiech M, Felden C (2012) Big data – a state-of-the-art. In: Proceedings of AMCIS 2012, pp 1–11
2. Gartner Inc (2013) IT glossary big data. http://www.gartner.com/it-glossary/big-data. Accessed 28 June 2013
3. Bizer C, Boncz P, Brodie M (2011) The meaningful use of big data: four perspectives. SIGMOD 40(4):56–60
4. He Y, Lee R, Huai Y (2011) RCFile: a fast and space-efficient data placement structure in MapReduce-based warehouse systems. In: Proceedings of ICDE 2011, pp 1199–1208
5. Simmhan Y, Barga R, Heasley J (2009) GrayWulf: scalable software architecture for data intensive computing. In: Proceedings of HICSS 2009, pp 1–10
6. Miles M, Huberman A (1994) Qualitative data analysis. Sage, Thousand Oaks
7. Flick U (2009) An introduction to qualitative research. Sage, London
8. Glaser B, Strauss A (1967) The discovery of grounded theory. Aldine Transaction, Chicago
9. Glaser B (1978) Theoretical sensitivity: advances in the methodology of grounded theory. Sociology Press, Mill Valley
10. Cooper H (1998) Synthesizing research: a guide for literature reviews. Sage, Thousand Oaks
11. Hughes J, Jones S (2003) Reflections on the use of grounded theory in interpretive information systems research. In: Proceedings of ECIS 2003, paper 62
12. Hughes J, Wood-Harper T (1999) Systems development as a research act. J Inf Technol 14 (1):83–94
13. Strauss A, Corbin J (1990) Basics of qualitative research: grounded theory procedures and techniques. Sage, Thousand Oaks
14. Gluchowski P, Gabriel R, Dittmar C (2008) Management support systeme und business intelligence. Springer, Berlin
15. Hackathorn R (2012) Current practices in active data warehousing. DM review, white paper
16. Chen H, Chiang R, Storey V (2012) Business intelligence and analytics: from big data to big impact. MIS Q 36(4):1165–1188
17. Grant R (1996) Prospering in dynamically-competitive environments: organizational capability as knowledge integration. Organ Sci 7(4):375–387
18. Barney J, Wright M, David J, Ketchen J (2001) The resource-based view of the firm: ten years after 1991. J Manag 27(6):625–641
19. Alavi M, Leidner D (2001) Review: knowledge management and knowledge management systems. MIS Q 25(1):107–136
20. Krumm J, Davies N, Narayanaswami C (2008) User-generated content. Pervasive Comput 7 (4):10–11
21. Monash C (2010) Three broad categories of data. http://www.dbms2.com/2010/01/17/three-broad-categories-of-data. Accessed 8 July 2013
22. Bitincka L, Ganapathi A, Zhang S (2012) Experiences with workload management in Splunk. In: Proceedings of MBDS 2012, pp 25–30
23. DiNucci D (1999) Fragmented future. Print 53:32–35
24. Borkar V, Carey M, Li C (2012) Inside "big data management". In: Proceedings of EDBT/ICDT 2012, pp 3–14
25. Kaplan A, Haenlein M (2010) Users of the world, unite! The challenges and opportunities of Social Media. Bus Horizons 53(1):59–68
26. IBM Coop (2013) What is big data. http://www-01.ibm.com/software/data/bigdata. Accessed 10 July 2013
27. Sterling T, Stark D (2009) A high-performance computing forecast: partly cloudy. Comput Sci Eng 11(4):42–49
28. Freedman D, Kisilev P (2009) Fast mean shift by compact density representation. In: Proc CVPR recognition 2009, pp 1818–1825

29. Dean J, Ghemawat S (2004) MapReduce: simplified data processing on large clusters. In: Proceedings of OSDI, pp 137–149
30. Krcmar H (2012) Information management. Springer, Berlin
31. Li X, Lillibridge M, Uysal M (2010) Reliability analysis of deduplicated and erasure-coded storage. Proc SIGMETRICS 38(3):4–9
32. Fayyad U, Piatetsky-Shapiro G, Smyth P (1996) From data mining to knowledge discovery: an overview. In: Fayyad U, Piatetsky-Shapiro G, Smyth P, Uthurusamy R (eds) Advances in knowledge discovery and data mining. AAAI Press, Menlo Park, pp 37–54
33. Miner G, Delen D, Fast A, Eider J (2012) Practical text mining and statistical analysis for non-structured text data. Academic, Waltham
34. Wagner L, Van Belle J (2007) Web mining for strategic intelligence: South African experiences and a practical methodology. In: Proceedings of ICDSS 2007, paper 1
35. Lukashevich H, Nowak S, Dunker P (2009) Using one-class SVM outliers detection for verification of collaboratively tagged image training sets. In: Proceedings of ICME 2009, pp 682–685
36. Wasserman S, Faust K (1994) Social network analysis: methods and applications, structural analysis. Cambridge University Press, New York
37. Shmueli G, Koppius O (2011) Predictive analytics in information systems research. MIS Q 35 (3):553–572
38. Balsa Rodriguez M, Gobbetti E, Guitian M (2013) A survey of compressed GPU-based direct volume rendering. In: Proceedings of Eurographics 2013
39. Hartmann S (1996) The world as a process: simulations in the natural and social sciences. In: Hegselmann R, Mueller U, Troitzsch K (eds) Modeling and simulation in the social sciences from the philosophy of science point of view. Kluwer Academic, Dordrecht, pp 77–100
40. Chailan R, Bouchette F, Dumontier C (2012) High performance pre-computing: prototype application to a coastal flooding decision tool. Knowledge and systems engineering (KSE). In: Proceedings of KSE 2012, pp 195–202
41. Buhl H, Röglinger M, Moser F, Heidemann J (2013) Big data – a fashionable topic with(out) sustainable relevance for research and practice? Bus Inf Syst Eng 5(2):65–69
42. Kohlwey E, Sussman A, Trost J (2011) Leveraging the cloud for big data biometrics. In: Proceedings of world congress services 2011, pp 597–601
43. Zimbra D, Chen H (2011) Stakeholder approach to stock prediction using finance social media. In: Chen H (ed) Intelligent systems smart market and money. IEEE, Washington, DC, pp 88–92
44. Toole J, Eagle N, Plotkin J (2011) Spatiotemporal correlations in criminal offense records. ACM Trans Intell Syst Technol 2(4), article 38
45. Venkataraman S, Tolia N, Ranganathan P (2011) Consistent and durable data structures for non-volatile byte- addressable memory. In: Proceedings of USENIX 2011, pp 1–15
46. Zhang Y, Gong B, Hui Liu Y (2011) Parallel option pricing with BSDEs method on MapReduce. In: Proceedings of ICCRD, pp 289–293
47. TechAmerica, Foundation Big Data Commission (2013) http://www.techamericafoundation.org/bigdata. Accessed 28 Oct 2013

Business Intelligence 2.0

Sebastian Behrendt and Alexander Richter

Abstract The increasing use of enterprise social networks (ESN) generates vast amounts of data, giving researchers and managerial decision makers unprecedented opportunities for analysis. However, more transparency about the available data dimensions and how these can be combined is needed to yield accurate insights into the multi-facetted phenomenon of ESN use. In order to address this issue, we present a framework of available data dimensions and describe possible methods and insights as well as opportunities and limitations of each data dimension. We then adopt this framework exemplary to comprehensively analyze an empirical ESN case.

Keywords Enterprise social networks • Social software • Social network analysis • Data dimensions • Mixed methods • Case study

1 New Opportunities

Work culture within and between enterprises is subject to constant changes towards more flexibility, especially in the sense of location- and time-independent work [1, 2]. In the context of changing communication and collaboration practices, systems that support connected and distributed work, such as Enterprise Social Networks (ESN), play an increasingly important role. They facilitate the generation of large quantities of user generated content [3, 4] and simultaneously lead to a high degree of interconnectivity among a companys' employees [5, 6]. Since almost every interaction in the system leaves a persistent digital trace [7], the increasing use of ESN produces a considerable amount of data. This "revolution in the measurement of collective human behavior" [8, p. 66] gives researchers and managerial decision makers unprecedented opportunities to analyze and explain such systems. In this context Chen et al. [9] use the term "Business Intelligence 2.0" to emphasize that

S. Behrendt (✉)
Bundeswehr University, Neubiberg, Germany
e-mail: s.behrendt@unibw.de

A. Richter
University of Zurich, Zurich, Switzerland
e-mail: arichter@ifi.uzh.ch

J.H. Mayer, R. Quick (eds.), *Business Intelligence for New-Generation Managers*,
DOI 10.1007/978-3-319-15696-5_8

the type of data analyzed is user generated and structured differently from other systems for BPM, CRM or ERP.

Yet, there seems to be a lack of transparency about the available options and likely implications of concrete decisions on the sources that should be adopted in an analysis. Therefore, in this chapter we pick up the keyword "Business Intelligence 2.0" and explain which methods can be applied to analyze ESN and which questions can be answered by doing so.

Our chapter in particular informs and supports people who are responsible for the introduction and implementation of an ESN or similar systems for communication and collaboration. We furthermore want to address users who can profit from the added value of an ESN by a constant evaluation of best practices in their daily business. Due to these various requirements different metrics and methods need to be applied jointly.

2 Overview of Types of Data and Analysis Methods

In the following we will present different types of data and associated analysis methods. Data on user interactions on such a platform are for example saved in log files and provide information about the extent of usage (*usage data*). Additionally, the users generated content, e.g. in the form of written text or images, can be analyzed (*user-generated data*). Moreover, connections between users are established as soon as users interact with one another, e.g., by "following" others or answering to previous posts (*structural data*). With time, users get a picture about the platform itself and make their own experiences (*user perception*). In the following we will describe each dimension in detail, including possible insights, data collection approaches and a short discussion of each data dimension.

2.1 Activities

As soon as someone uses an ESN, a digital trace is left behind. Almost all functions within such a system create *usage data,* which is collected by cookies, log files, page tagging, web beacons, and packet sniffing [10]. Alternatively, direct access to the underlying databases can facilitate its export. This covers quantitative and partly accumulated data, such as:

- accessed web pages and frequency of visits,
- the number of downloads and origin of visitors (locations),
- the time stamp and duration,
- the amount of created/edited content (most often divided into different types of content like status message, comment, blog entry, etc.) and also

- the number of groups created (divided into different types of groups, e.g., open, closed, etc.).

Goal of the Analysis

The analysis of usage data does not only provide an overview of the usage intensity of the ESN, but allows drawing conclusions on what content was accessed by whom, when, how often, and for how long. It sheds light on key activity areas of the platform and helps to identify how many registered users are really active and how many stay rather passive. The differentiation of different types of content and groups enables, among other things, the identification of most preferred content, most active groups and whether conversations are held rather openly or privately. Depending on the functional range of the platform advanced analyses are possible too, for example, the number of questions that were actually answered or the amount of time passed until a response was posted. These data can be evaluated in order to understand the technologies in use, or to improve the design and usability, to accelerate content updates, or even to improve the website's performance. Figure 1 shows exemplarily the temporal development of user statistics and the development of different content types.

Possible Approach

Already for quite some time it is common to log user actions on web pages in various ways (so-called web tracking). Usage data are either stored on the server (in the form of log files) or on the user device (e.g., by JavaScript tags, by so-called count pixels or by cookies) after which they can be analyzed and then visualized by different web-analytics tools. Likewise, this procedure can be applied to ESNs. Detailed data, such as the number of different contents, are often provided by the ESN itself and are most often aggregated and visualized via some kind of dashboard. For further processing (like for example the above image, created with Microsoft Excel) an export to the desired format is necessary. A significant advantage is that this data can be exported at any time and across any timeframe (depending on the platform settings). However, organizational events and constraints need to be considered as well. For example a community managers' promotion of certain topics, or the presentation of important organizational communiqué can influence this data indirectly.

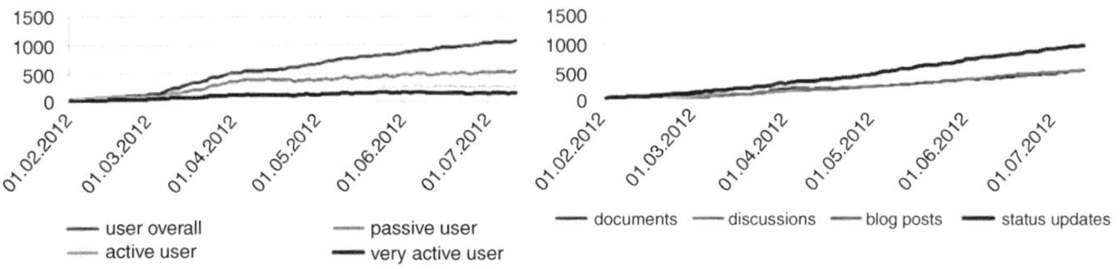

Fig. 1 Possible representation of usage data

Discussion
Usage data are logged automatically and continuously by the different mechanisms. Due to the fact that the tools often provide data in an already pre-processed way, an analysis is possible without much effort (see e.g., Yammer in Sect. 3). Furthermore, data can be processed graphically in order to quickly and easily show changes over time. Nevertheless, analysis possibilities depend both on the web tracking tools used and the ESN itself. If certain actions are not logged, it is almost impossible to retrieve them later on, or at least it requires additional effort to retrieve them, e.g., with the help of own tracking mechanisms. Similarly, the export of this data for further use in other tools (e.g., Excel) may be restricted or require a lot of effort.

2.2 Content

Although usage data provides information on the amount and distribution of activity on a given website, it hardly allows for any conclusions on why users have visited the platform, whether they have achieved their goals, and if the platform was useful in this respect. In order to better understand and interpret these activities, it is helpful to take a closer look at *user-generated data*.

Some examples for these are:

- status messages, blog entries, and comments,
- appointments & tasks or
- wiki pages.

Goal of the Analysis
Insights accessible via an analysis of user-generated content can be of very different type and can be achieved via various methods including content analysis, sentiment analysis, text mining, or genre analysis. Content analysis tries to draw replicable conclusions from textual data to its context [11], it allows automatic discovery of new, previously unknown information [12]. Hence, a content analysis can identify topics that are currently being discussed intensively or extract communication practices of users. This illustrates how and for what purpose the ESN is used. Sentiment analysis aims to determine a person's attitude towards a specific topic [13]. Hence it is possible to discern the employees' mood, so-called sentiments, between the lines of written text. By taking network structures into consideration, it is even possible to make statements about distribution patterns of sentiments within an organization [14]. These distribution processes develop as people are influenced by the emotional state of other participants during electronic communication [14, 15]. Text mining allows for discovering new information in written communication, or finding patterns across datasets [12] by using linguistic, statistical, and machine learning techniques. In a genre analysis, one or more communication genres are manually assigned to each content element corresponding to their purpose. Communication genres are "socially recognized types of communicative

actions [. . .] which are habitually executed by members of a community and which pursue a defined social goal" [16]. They are therefore well suited to describe communication practices and usage patterns within groups. For example Riemer and Richter [17] conducted a genre analysis of an enterprise social network and found that its usage in the enterprise context differed greatly from that in the private context. Usage was more work-related than some upper managers expected. Unwanted behavior, like non-work-related chatter, does not automatically emerge when social technologies are applied in the enterprise environment.

Summarizing, by analyzing the content, it is possible to verify if the ESN is used the way it was planned at the time of introduction or if new (even better) ways of use have evolved.

Possible Approach

In order to analyze user-generated content effectively, an export of selected content is necessary. This can be realized either via a platform's own export function, by RSS feeds or directly via the underlying data base. After an appropriate processing of the data, which often includes anonymization of users, text mining methods can be used to analyze the data. In the following, genre analysis and sentiment analysis shall be presented as examples.

Sentiment analysis Besides functional content, a user also communicates sensations, feelings or opinions, e.g., about a certain product, a person or an issue. These sensations are called sentiments and can be extracted from unstructured texts [13]. Apart from the actual parameter value (positive/negative), the strength of the respective value can be determined or peculiarities of textual communication like emoticons, abbreviations or sarcasm can be considered [18, 19].

Genre analysis During a genre analysis content is analyzed manually with the aim of identifying certain ways of communication that are regularly used by a group and serve a defined social purpose [16]. Every type of content is attributed one or more genres of communication in the process. Figure 2 shows an exemplary result of a genre analysis where, in this case, the platform serves mainly for the exchange of opinions, but less so for the generation of ideas.

Discussion

Both methods deliver qualitative results and allow a better understanding of user behavior. Since the analysis is based on unstructured data, the results will always be subject to errors or a certain indetermination. This affects both the automated and manual analysis, because human interpretation of a text also allows different opinions and while analyzing large numbers errors can never be completely eliminated. Differences are especially visible in the amount of effort necessary. An automated text analysis may require certain preparatory (structuring) measures, such as PoS tagging, categorization or grouping [12]. Manual analysis, on the other hand, requires reading and a good understanding of the texts. Here, the size of a text can quickly become a restriction and the analysis is subject to a larger time delay. Consequently, a continuous evaluation becomes very difficult and can only be handled by random sampling or respectively over a fixed span of time.

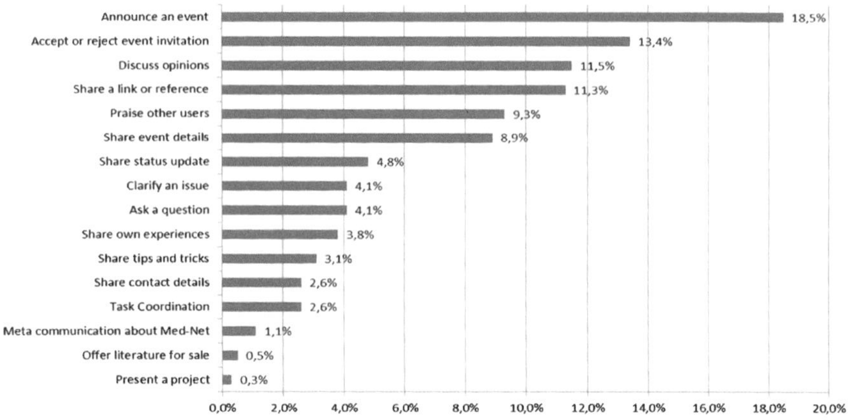

Fig. 2 Distribution of possible genres of communication

2.3 Relations

As soon as users of an ESN interact with one another, relations develop between them, the so-called *structural data*. The study of the connection between different persons, the so-called network analysis (SNA), has been common practice in social sciences for a long time [20]. However, in the social sciences, these relations were often created manually, for example, by means of interviews, which is a painstakingly slow process. While using an ESN, connections of all kinds develop automatically the moment users interact in any way on the platform. Be it by commenting, rating or linking the entry of another user or by following or becoming friends with someone (depending on the platform features). Hence, connections are established between two persons, between a person and content, or even between different contents.

Goal of the Analysis

Basically, a SNA provides insights into the structure of analyzed objects and into how they are related to one another, or whether certain patterns exist. If a network analysis is not only performed at a certain point of time, but over a span of time, this allows to discover developments within the network, so-called network dynamics [21]. If it is also possible to determine the directivity of a relation, statements about action and reaction within a network become possible (e.g., user A follows user B, whereupon user B decides to follow user A).

Based on the fundamental metrics of network analysis like centrality and density [22] statements are possible on:

- how fast information spreads within a network,
- how the actions of different users affect the information exchange,
- or how important or visible certain actors are in the network.

Starting from the original analytic aims in sociology it can be determined how people communicate with one another. In this way, companies can analyze their own communication structures and identify, e.g., bottlenecks or dependencies. According to [23], a different perspective on communication is also possible. The authors differentiate between a "conventional" view of "communication *in* organizations" (i.e. how communication takes place within organizations) and another view, namely that communication *constitutes* an organization. Based on this perspective, statements can be made, e.g., on how communication influences the organizational structure or on how the predefined formal structure of a company (e.g., defined in terms of an organization chart) differs from the so-called informal structure (defined by unplanned relations and interactions between employees). For executives, this offers the possibility to identify and understand the true nature of collaboration in their organization, and hence to better support it [24].

Possible Approach

In order to evaluate these relations a social network analysis (SNA) is well suited. In social sciences a network analysis according to Freeman [25] is characterized by four criteria:

1. the analysis of social relations between actors as an important element of social order,
2. the systematic collection and analysis of empirical data,
3. the graphical representation of this data, and
4. mathematical and computer-aided formal models to obtain abstractions of this data.

Data obtained in this way can be visualized, e.g., as a graph (cf. Fig. 3). A graph in this sense is a set of vertices (often also called nodes) representing the actors in the network paired with a set of edges (often also called ties) that represent relations between actors [26].

To establish connections or a graph it is necessary to clearly formulate the analytical focus. This determines which actors need to be considered and how the relationship developing between them will be defined. Consequently, the required data need to be exported from the ESN and processed. The analysis or visualization is facilitated by different tools like R[1] or Commetrix.[2]

Discussion

A social network analysis shows connections that are not visible using other analysis methods. However, the method can produce various results, which is why it is important to clearly define the analytical focus beforehand. This not only determines the definition of actors and relationships, but also relevant metrics and visualization types.

[1] http://www.r-project.org

[2] http://www.commetrix.de

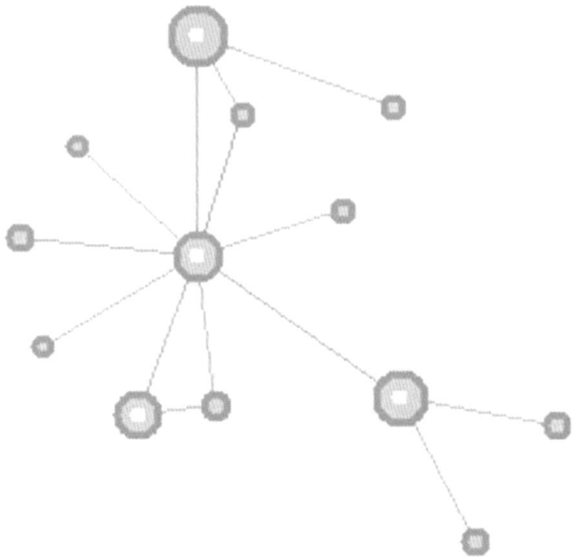

Fig. 3 Graph representation of a network

2.4 Experiences

With time users make different experiences with the ESN. This has a large influence on how they perceive the system. Hence, they develop their own view or respectively their own opinion about the ESN (*user perception*). Users' experience of and the attitude they develop when using a platform provide insights into their experiential life [27]. Still, they hardly ever communicate it explicitly via messages in the ESN.

Goal of the Analysis

The data treated so far offer an objective (within the limits of what is possible) view on the events in the ESN. Interviews or surveys allow gathering subjective impressions of persons involved and improve the understanding of user practices. Practice has pointed out that companies show particular interest in statements on use and optimization potential (cf. Table 1). Especially the use (for the company) of an ESN comes within reach by this method, as it is rather difficult to quantify the economic value of such a system due to its malleable character [28].

Possible Approach

In order to determine usage practices it is necessary to ask the users directly about them. One way to do this is in the form of interviews or questionnaires. The latter are well suited to collect answers for precise questions in a large scale and can be conducted online, e.g., in the company's own intranet or respectively directly in the ESN. Interviews, on the contrary, are well suited to collect qualitatively better responses and obtain personal opinions or to drill down on certain topics. Both methods require the definition of concrete questions beforehand based on which an

Table 1 Benefits of an ESN

Use	Optimization potential	Usage practices
Employee satisfaction (due to the new type of communication) Time savings (e.g., to find necessary information for problem solutions) Content quality Cost savings (e.g., by lower travel costs)	Satisfaction with the ESN Problems while using the ESN	Aim of using the ESN Identification of concrete use cases and best practices

interview guideline or an online survey is created. The evaluation of interviews is performed manually to a large degree since the given responses need to be interpreted correctly.

Discussion
The collection of such qualitative data offers a good way to triangulate the results obtained so far from other data dimensions. They render the data more tangible by supplying the necessary context, albeit only as a selective survey. Similar to the social network analysis, interviews or questionnaires can provide many different results. They demand good preparation and are very time-consuming (preparation, execution, analysis). This also includes ensuring the compliance with data privacy policies and company agreements, e.g., by integrating the works council at an early stage. Equally, it is necessary to grant employees enough time for participation parallel to their full working day and to handle results transparently at all times. Table 2 gives a summarizing overview about each data dimension.

3 Mix of Methods in Practical Application

All methods treated so far allow different insights and have individual strengths and weaknesses which we want to illustrate with two examples from practice.

For the first example we take a look at the cloud-based enterprise social network "Yammer", which is currently being used by more than 200,000 companies according to their own declaration and which was taken over by Microsoft in the summer of 2012. For several years Yammer has been offering simple and clear statistics on *usage data* that provide every user with an overview of activities in their network. One of the things to mention is the growth of the network over a certain span of time, measured by new members, and messages. Moreover, Yammer analyzes the number of actually active members that performed an action at least once in that time—be it only changing between two different group feeds. Additionally, there is information about the five most active groups as well as the most popular ways of access (e.g., web client or mobile app) (Fig. 4).

On top of that, Yammer offers the so-called "leader boards" wherein, for a certain span of time, the most active (in terms of messages) or most popular

Table 2 Data dimension overview

Data dimensions	Characteristics	Exemplary data collection methods	Exemplary data analysis methods
Activities (usage data)	Data can originate from various sources The automatic collection results in an extensive amount of data The quantity and quality of an analysis depend on the features of the underlying system, the export options, and the complexity of the database structure	Log files; Tracking pixel; cookies	Web analytics
Content (user generated data)	Is documented in a corresponding context / related communication (threads) Requires manual preparation (e.g., data selection or pre-processing) Can be analyzed manually or automatically Allows for subjective bias in manual analysis Supports multilingual settings	Structured content export	Genre analysis; Sentiment analysis; Text mining; Content analysis
Relations (relational data)	Different types of relations Are affected by platform features and intended tie design Allow for the analysis of network dynamics and evolution	Structured content export	SNA; Dynamic network analysis
Experiences (perceptional data)	Must be documented manually and sporadically Can be assessed on a sample basis only Allow for a deeper understanding of user intensions and the underlying context Require a huge effort to prepare, conduct, and analyze Allow for subjective bias in the collection and analysis process	Interviews; Questionnaires	Content analysis

(in terms of "Likes") users as well as further personal activity indices are shown. This approach on the one hand clearly targets "gamification", but on the other hand also helps identifying influencers within the network.

As explained above, these automated analyses of usage data do not shed light on contents actually exchanged. Therefore, a study published in 2010 qualitatively analyzed more than 1,000 messages over Yammer at Capgemini with the help of a genre analysis [29]. Identified usage patterns show how and for what purpose employees use Yammer, in this case mostly for discussions and problem solutions. Hence, they provide insights into how the ESN supports collaboration at Capgemini

Fig. 4 Automatic processing of usage data in Yammer

and show the role and added value of the platform inside the company. Furthermore, personal interviews with selected users were conducted for the study in order to learn more about the motivation and current challenges using Yammer in the company.

The second example deals with the evaluation of the "San-Netz", an online social network for training medical officers of the German armed forces comprising 1,200 registered members at the moment of evaluation [30]. The applied mix of methods was used to analyze all above mentioned data dimensions, i.e. qualitative and quantitative methods were combined.

For the *analysis of the usage* data 23 months were taken into consideration. Here, it was mainly interesting to see a major part of topic-focused communication take place in groups with restricted access. General knowledge exchange, on the contrary, was in areas open to all members. The frequency analysis of different types of content showed surprisingly many contents of the type "*appointment*" (33 %) which was confirmed by the *genre analysis*. Here, 1,155 messages from 204 users in 5 selected San-Netz groups were analyzed. With a 44 % share *coordination of meetings* was the major part of communication. This clearly shows that a mix of methods can confirm the result of a single method.

The conducted *interview study*[3] came to the conclusion that the hierarchy of the German armed forces (respectively the military structure) barely affects communication. It was even said that the threshold to address a higher rank is lower in San-Netz than it is, e.g., in the barracks. However, the *social network analysis*[4] yielded contradictory results. Here, it became evident that hardly any hierarchy-spanning

[3] 13 Interviews with officers/officer candidates from different ranked were conducted.

[4] Analysis of 445 connections based on 1,155 messages by 204 users

- Nodes: users that generated a content, e.g., appointment, blog, article, comment
- Edges: comments on initial contents

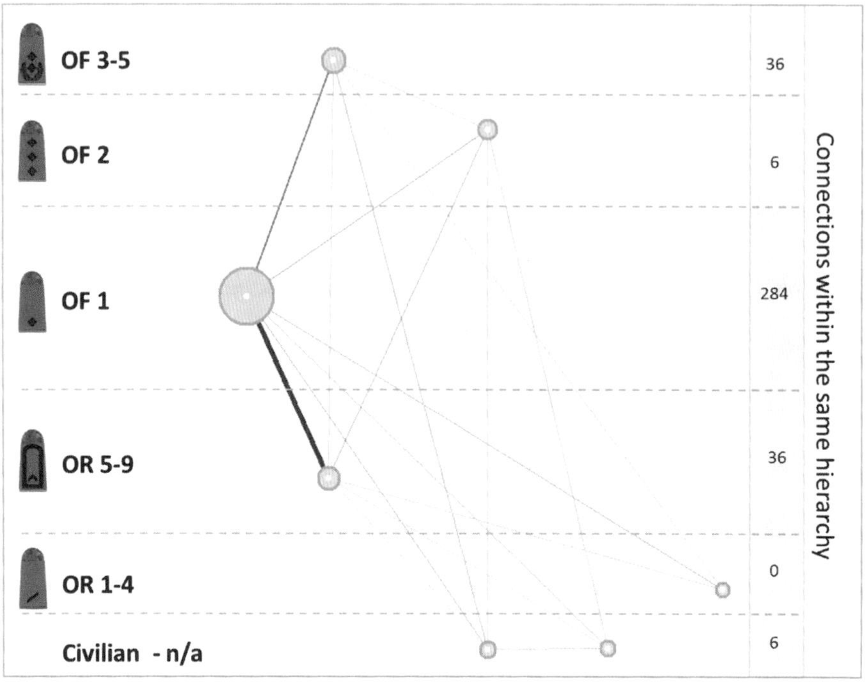

Fig. 5 Illustration of rank-spanning networking

networking takes place. There even emerged so-called bridgeheads in that lieutenants formed a connection between higher and lower ranks, as can be seen in Fig. 5.

Moreover, the SNA showed an uneven distribution of connections as there are only a few people keeping the network together. Although the analysis of usage data already showed that certain people create particularly many contents, only the additional social network analysis revealed the role of these people for the network stability. The usage data also showed that there were certain points of time where more users joined the platform. All of this clearly shows that the results of some methods on their own lack the explanatory power to correctly understand the events inside the ESN. Only by means of data triangulation [31] it becomes possible to increase the explanatory power of the gained insights. In this way, the distribution, conditions, and consequences of patterns of action or network practices can be investigated and a comprehensive picture of social phenomena can be drawn [32]. In the case of the San-Netz the individual analysis results partly confirmed results of other methods. However, they also revealed contradictions in that, for example, the impressions that users get from using the network substantially differ from the measured "reality". This shows that such a mixed methods approach is a suitable means to obtain a more realistic picture of such a network. Summarizing, a mixed method approach can yield four distinct effects [30]: the mutual confirmation of results, the detection of conflicting results, the clarification of observed phenomena and the revelation of new insights.

4 Conclusion

The communication inside a connected organization makes a wide range of different data (Activities, Content, Relations, Experiences) available for analysis. The applicable analytical methods and the questions that these analyses can answer are equally diverse. We argued that a mixed methods analytic approach can produce better results than a single method approach, because it considers combinations of different sources of evidence. A mixed methods approach is not only applicable to the evaluation of an ESN for research, but it also creates additional value for organizational decision makers, as the evaluation results are more significant and more comprehensive. Hence, the analysis of these four data dimensions yields valuable insights for relevant business decisions. Yet, just because it is *possible* to analyze almost anything it is not *necessary* to actually do so. The analysis of an ESN should be preceded by a concrete question or respectively a goal based on which required metrics are identified and an approach is developed. This step bears a certain liability for persons responsible for the platform. Especially the evaluation should help improve the understanding of structures and processes inside the organization; however, it should not support the surveillance of individual employees by means of personal data. In this context, requirements of data security and active company agreements play an important role. It is necessary to develop techniques for anonymization which comply with individual people's rights, but simultaneously answer the company's questions as good as possible. If generally only an analysis in aggregated form is possible (e.g. without a possible identification of single users), the possibilities to analyze cross-links or typical user profiles cease to exist, e.g., "users active in group X are also mostly active in group Z".

While analyzing collected data it is always important to consider the context of use [20] in order to be able and interpret the data correctly. This can either be the context of the use case of interest or the general guidelines for using the ESN. Therefore interviews are a suitable means, as they enable researchers to reveal the required context. A mix of methods in this regard also offers the possibility to investigate how certain communication patterns influence network structures (or vice versa). In particular the combination of content analysis and social network analysis can help substantially improve the understanding of communication and collaboration processes in organizations as they offer the possibility to detect informal employee networks.

Finally, we want to point out that in companies currently not only available data are subject to change, but also *how* they are analyzed. Most notably a trend should be mentioned, towards an increasing prominence of "self-service business intelligence" or "BI as-a-service", that is the possibility to perform analyses individually and flexibly without being dependent on direct support by the IT department, which is offered by the tools and correspondingly requested by the operating departments. Moreover, modern BI tools more and more become collaborative environments and increasingly offer features for simple distributed or, where necessary, time-displaced collaboration. For example, generated reports can easily be commented or discussed or statuses during an analysis can be bookmarked and shared with other people. Hence, the trend is clearly towards a joint data analysis using the possibilities of increasing interconnectivity, which in turn, provides enough space for future research.

References

1. Majumdar A, Krishna S, Bjorn P (2013) Managers' perceptions of social software use in the workplace: identifying the benefits of social software and emerging patterns of its use. In: Proceedings of the 19th Americas conference on information systems (AMCIS), Chicago
2. Kaiser S, Kozica A (2014) Über Grenzverschiebungen in der neuen, vernetzten Arbeitswelt. In: Richter A (ed) Vernetzte organisation. Oldenbourg Wissenschaftsverlag, München, pp 7–15
3. Richter A, Riemer K (2013) Malleable end-user software. Bus Inf Syst Eng 5(3):195–197
4. Richter A, Koch M (2008) Funktionen von social-networking-diensten. In: Bichler M, Hess T, Krcmar H et al. (eds) World wide web internet and web information systems, vol 2008. Gito, pp 1239–1250
5. Riemer K, Richter A (2010) Tweet Inside: microblogging in a corporate context. In: Proceedings 23rd Bled eConference eTrust: implications for the individual, enterprises and society
6. Trier M, Richter A (2014) The deep structure of organizational online networking. An actor-oriented case study. Inf Syst J. doi:10.1111/isj.12047
7. Aral S, Dellarocas C, Godes D (2013) Introduction to the special issue—social media and business transformation: a framework for research. Inf Syst Res 24(1):3–13
8. Kleinberg J (2008) The convergence of social and technological networks. Commun ACM 51 (11):66–72
9. Chen H, Chiang RHL, Storey VC (2012) Business intelligence and analytics: from big data to big impact. MIS Q 36(4):1165–1188
10. Kumar L, Singh H, Kaur R (2012) Web analytics and metrics: a survey. In: Proceedings of the international conference on advances in computing, communications and informatics. ACM, New York, pp 966–971
11. Krippendorff K (2013) Content analysis. An introduction to its methodology, 3rd edn. Sage, London
12. Ben-Dov M, Feldman R (2005) Text mining and information extraction. In: Maimon O, Rokach L (eds) Data mining and knowledge discovery handbook. Springer, New York, pp 801–831
13. Pang B, Lee L, Aggarwal CC et al (2008) Opinion Mining and Sentiment Analysis. Found Trends Inf Retr 2(2):1–135
14. Hillmann R, Trier M (2012) Dissemination patterns and associated network effects of sentiments in social networks. In: 2012 IEEE/ACM international conference on advances in social networks analysis and mining
15. Christakis NA, Fowler JH (2009) Connected. The surprising power of our social networks and how they shape our lives, 1st edn. Little, Brown and Co, New York

16. Yates J, Orlikowski WJ, Okamura K (1999) Explicit and implicit structuring of genres in electronic communication: reinforcement and change of social interaction. Organ Sci 10(1):83–103
17. Riemer K, Richter A (2010) Social software: agents for change or platforms for social reproduction? A case study on enterprise microblogging. In: Proceedings of the 21th Australasian conference on information systems, Brisbane
18. Thelwall M, Buckley K, Paltoglou G et al (2010) Sentiment strength detection in short informal text. J Am Soc Inf Sci 61(12):2544–2558
19. Davidov D, Tsur O, Rappoport A (2010) Semi-supervised recognition of sarcastic sentences in Twitter and Amazon. In: Proceedings of the fourteenth conference on computational natural language learning, pp 107–116
20. Schnegg M (2010) Die Wurzeln der Netzwerkforschung. In: Stegbauer C, Häußling R (eds) Handbuch Netzwerkforschung. VS Verlag für Sozialwissenschaften, Wiesbaden
21. Trier M (2010) Struktur und Dynamik in der Netzwerkanalyse. In: Stegbauer C, Häußling R (eds) Handbuch Netzwerkforschung. VS Verlag für Sozialwissenschaften, Wiesbaden, pp 205–217
22. Jansen D (1999) Einführung in die Netzwerkanalyse. VS Verlag für Sozialwissenschaften, Wiesbaden
23. Blaschke S, Schoeneborn D, Seidl D (2012) Organizations as networks of communication episodes: turning the network perspective inside out. Organ Stud 33(7):879–906
24. Allen J, James AD, Gamlen P (2007) Formal versus informal knowledge networks in R&D: a case study using social network analysis. R&D Manag 37(3):179–196
25. Freeman LC (2004) The development of social network analysis: a study in the sociology of science. Empirical Press, Vancouver
26. Brandes U (2010) Graphentheorie. In: Stegbauer C, Häußling R (eds) Handbuch Netzwerkforschung. VS Verlag für Sozialwissenschaften, Wiesbaden
27. Schultze U, Avital M (2011) Designing interviews to generate rich data for information systems research. Inf Organ 21(1):1–16
28. Richter A, Heidemann J, Klier M et al (2013) Success measurement of enterprise social networks. Tagungsband Wirtschaftsinformatik, In
29. Riemer K, Richter A, Bohringer M (2010) Enterprise microblogging. Wirtschaftsinformatik 52(6):387–390
30. Behrendt S, Richter A, Trier M (2014) Mixed methods analysis of enterprise social networks. Comput Netw. doi:10.1016/j.comnet.2014.08.025
31. Denzin NK (1970) The research act in sociology: a theoretical introduction to sociological methods, Methodological perspectives. Butterworth, London
32. Hollstein B (2010) Qualitative methoden und mixed-method-designs. In: Stegbauer C, Häußling R (eds) Handbuch Netzwerkforschung. VS Verlag für Sozialwissenschaften, Wiesbaden, pp 459–470

Self-Service Management Support Systems: Findings from a New-Generation Manager Perspective

Jörg H. Mayer, Jens Hartwig, André Röder, and Reiner Quick

Abstract New-generation managers are increasingly populating organizations' management. They consist of digital natives who grew up with Information Systems (IS) and digital immigrants who learned to engage with IS as adults. Today, such managers have to make faster decisions than in the past and find themselves more and more in mobile IS use situations. These requirements combined with managers' ability to use IS themselves result in the need for self-service Management Support Systems (MSS). This article develops a more business-driven design for such MSS. In doing so, we propose both a rigorous set of requirements and initial design guidelines to start further discussion. The utility of these guidelines is demonstrated with a "mobile-first" prototype on a modern business intelligence platform: the Corporate Navigator app.

Keywords New-generation managers • Management support systems (MSS) • Management reporting • Information systems (IS) analysis and design • Self-service IS • Principle of economic efficiency • Set of requirements • Design guidelines • Prototype • App design

1 Design Problem

The ability to make decisions on a rational basis about the "...configuration of resources within a changing environment, to meet the needs of markets and to fulfill stakeholder expectation" [1] distinguishes a *manager* from a knowledge worker [2].

Information Systems (IS) intended to help managers are known as *Management Support Systems (MSS)*. They have been a topic of research in the last 50 years [3–7] and serve as an for umbrella term for Management Information Systems (MIS),

J.H. Mayer (✉)
School of Management, University of St. Gallen, St. Gallen, Switzerland
e-mail: joerg.mayer@unisg.ch

J. Hartwig • A. Röder • R. Quick
Technische Universität Darmstadt, Darmstadt, Germany
e-mail: jens.hartwig@stud.tu-darmstadt.de; a.roeder@stud.tu-darmstadt.de; quick@bwl.tu-darmstadt.de

J.H. Mayer, R. Quick (eds.), *Business Intelligence for New-Generation Managers*, DOI 10.1007/978-3-319-15696-5_9

Decision Support Systems (DSS), Executive Information Systems (EIS), and more recently, Knowledge Management Systems (KMS) as well as Business Intelligence (BI) systems for managers [8, 9].

New-generation managers criticize MSS for their lack in accommodating their multifaceted work (functional requirements) and their individual attitude toward IS (non-functional requirements, [7, 10, 11]). They consist of both *digital natives* who grew up with IS as well as *digital immigrants* who learned to engage with IS as adults and developed into IS users over time [12].

From a *functional perspective* new-generation managers have significantly expanded their role in operations—in parallel to their strategic leadership. And they have to make decisions faster than in the past [13]. From a *non-functional perspective* they ask for better "IS design for use" [14]. Additionally, new-generation managers have to handle more and more *different IS use situations*, especially mobile situations such as traveling by train, plane or car with a driver [15].

These requirements combined with the managers' ability to use IS themselves result in the need for *self-service* MSS leveraging new IT-enablers—instead of relying on their assistants [16–18]. Among others, these IT-enablers include in-memory technology, which enables managers to see their data in real-time [19] and smart devices (e.g., tablets), which offer a convenient way to access the MSS—especially in mobile IS use situations [20].

Under these considerations, the objective of this article is to develop a more *business-driven MSS design*. Business-driven hereby means to consider not only what is technically possible, but what is economically feasible [21]. In doing so, we propose both a rigorous *set of requirements* and initial *design guidelines* to start further discussion. The utility of these guidelines is demonstrated with a "mobile-first" prototype on a modern BI platform. We answer two research questions:

- What is a rigorous *set of requirements* handling the new-generation managers' need for self-service MSS?
- What are initial *design guidelines* for such a MSS design to start further discussion and are these guidelines useful in practice?

Following the emerging tenets of design science research (DSR) in IS [22], we follow a six-step process model by Peffers et al. [23]. Sect. 1 motivates the research by introducing new-generation managers and their requirements for a self-service MSS leveraging new IT-enablers. Then, the under-lying research model and findings from a literature research are discussed and summarized in a set of requirements for self-service MSS (Sect. 2). By applying these requirements in a multi-case study, design guidelines are developed from the findings (Sect. 3). Their utility is demonstrated with a "mobile-first" prototype on a modern BI platform (Sect. 4). The evaluation covers both the DSR in IS process and the developed artefact of initial design guidelines (Sect. 5). Finally, we conclude with a summary, limitations and avenues for future research. This work is based on our prior work which presented the set of requirements [21] and exposed the prototype [24].

2 Requirements Analysis

2.1 Literature Review

We followed vom Brocke et al.'s [25] four step process for literature research and focused on leading IS research outlets provided by the London School of Economics [26]. We reviewed the outlets via AIS Electronic Library, EBSCO host, ProQuest and a standard Google search was used to cover recent contributions from practice [21].

A first keyword search, focused on MSS and management reporting, led to unsatisfactory results in terms of quantity and quality to start our research. As a consequence we did both expanding our journal base with six high impact accounting journals and complementing our search string with "management accounting system," "management accounting," and "schedule". The final search string (see Fig. 1) applied on the new journal base yielded a total of 759 hits. After qualifying the titles and scanning the abstracts a final back and forward search led to 63 relevant publications overall (see Fig. 2).

The findings of our literature review expose the following shortcomings (Fig. 2, in detail, [38]):

(1) *Lack of MSS user requirements focusing on management reporting*. There are 28 publications regarding user requirements, but most of them do not focus on management reporting. For example, Tricker [27] describes manager information needs without stating specific reporting requirements. Both, Aders et al. [28] and Cheung and Babin [29] examine individual aspects for decision-making, such as the selection of relevant data sources and KPIs, but they do not incorporate these into a comprehensive MSS design. Furthermore, the researched list approaches lack a rigorous framework for requirements development [30]. In addition the researched requirements lists are most often outdated [5, 31] or do not cover the requirements of new-generation managers [32].

(2) *Lack of MSS design guidelines for management reporting applying new IT-enablers:* 14 out of 63 publications cover methods which describe how to

		OR					
AND		Management support system	Executive information system	Management accounting system	(Group) decision support system	Management information systems	Business intelligence
AND	OR	Schedule	Stakeholder	Recipients	Management board	Board of directors	
AND	OR	Management accounting	Requirements	Reporting	Report	Management	

Fig. 1 Keyword search string (taken from [21])

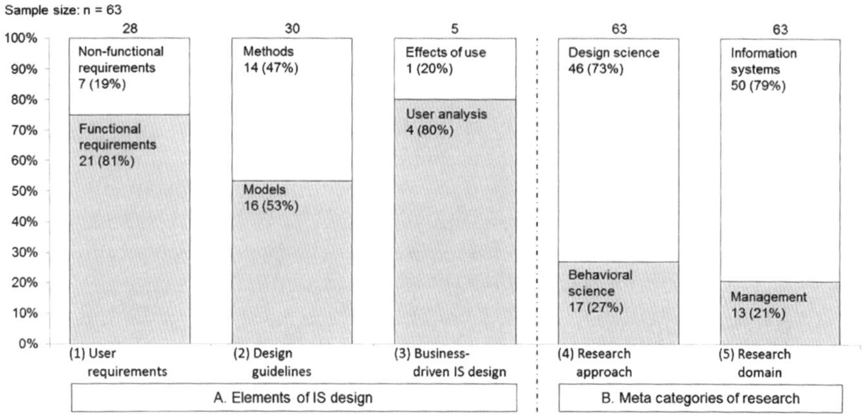

Fig. 2 Classification of the publications (taken from [21])

build MSS whereas 16 out of 63 publications focus on models. These publications provide insight into what information is reported and which methods such as environmental scanning are applied [33]. Nevertheless they neither cover how information should be presented nor how new IT-enablers can be applied accommodating new-generation managers user-group preferences. The only publication in which principles for MSS design based on a rigorous criteria list are derived is from [11], but they do not leverage new IT-enablers.

(3) *Business-driven IS design is comprehensive:* With only five publications covering business-driven IS design guidelines for MSS, we identified another gap. A configuration model accommodating different manager working styles was proposed by Mayer et al. [14]. Furthermore, Armstrong et al. [34] analyzed managers' cognitive styles and propose a better MSS design by using different modes of information presentation and the flexibility of interfaces for different working styles.

(4) *Research approaches could be more differentiated*: Three out of four publications applied DSR in IS. We propose twofold that more research should be conducted with a behavioral approach and that more artefacts in DSR in IS should be evaluated by the means of a multi-case study.

(5) *MSS with a focus on management reporting is covered neither in IS nor the management literature:* We examined only 13 publications in management literature on this topic. These publications only address external reporting to capital markets [35]. Publications covering the internal reporting only consider what should be reported [36, 37] and to whom [27], but do not develop concrete design guidelines.

Summarizing our findings, there is a lack of a rigorous, ready-to-use set of business-driven user requirements from a new-generation manager perspective. Additionally, design guidelines for designing self-service MSS are conspicuously absent as well.

Table 1 Set of requirements for MSS design and evaluation (taken from [21])

Principle of economic efficiency	Design criteria		Evaluation criteria			Description
Solution capabilities (IS output)	Strategic positioning (WHAT)	Purpose	EC	1	Stakeholder and complementary reports for additional recipients [27, 39]	Who are the recipients of the report? What is the coverage and volume of the reports?
	Conceptual design (HOW)	Content	EC	2	Key performance indicators (KPIs) [17, 28, 40]	What KPIs are primarily used? Are they traceable by a value-driver-tree?
			EC	3	Dimensions of analysis [17]	Which information clusters are covered? How are the performance indicators split up? What is their temporal reference?
			EC	4	Advanced performance management [33, 41, 42]	Which ancillary concepts are applied in the management reports? Compliance/risk management, environmental scanning? Exception reporting: Is it possible to define exceptions?
		Visualization	EC	5	Graphical design and data visualization [43–45]	How is the first "look&feel" and is the basic screen design consistent? How is the report's understandability? What kind of standard or advanced charts are used to visualize information?
		Process	EC	6	Reporting process [6]	When are which reports provided to recipients?

(continued)

Table 1 (continued)

Principle of economic efficiency	Design criteria		Evaluation criteria			Description
						When do the recipients discuss the reports?
	Business/IT-alignment	Flexibility	EC	7	Flexibility [14, 44]	How flexible is the MSS for accommodating individual information requirements and working styles?
	IT components (WHAT WITH)	New IT-enablers	EC	8	Mobile use scenarios [46, 47]	How comfortable is it to adapt stationary desktop design to smart devices (e.g., report transformation for smart devices)?
			EC	9	Different information media [48]	Are there different information media (paper, PDF, web, app) available to the recipients?
			EC	10	Collaboration/commenting [49, 50]	Is it possible to add comments to support collaboration across the company?
			EC	11	Real-time management [51, 52]	Is in-memory technology used to foster new kind of insights or faster processes?
			EC	12	Predictive analytics on big data [30, 53]	Are techniques from statistics, modeling, machine learning and data mining integrated into big data?
Resource requirements (IS input)	Effort	Adequacy	EC	13	Cost and time adequacy [54, 55]	What is the budget and time allocation for MSS design and implementation? What is the budget and time allocation for MSS operation and maintenance?

2.2 Set of Requirements

Combining the validity of SEMs and the relevance for practice of less rigorous list approaches, our research to derive requirements for MSS design follows a three-step approach [11, 21, 38] (see Table 1).

In the first step we choose the *principle of economic efficiency* to structure the upcoming MSS criteria. It is a generally accepted paradigm in business research [56] and addresses the ratio between benefit and cost. Thus, we are not guided by what is conceptually or technically possible but apply what is economically feasible. While the MSS benefits are measured in system capabilities, the general resource requirements are covered by the MSS costs.

In the second step, we specify the principle of economic efficiency into design criteria. We structure them by St.Gallen's Business Engineering approach [57] and Mayer's specification for MSS design [17, 38]. Applying this approach there are 4 + 1 design criteria: Strategic positioning, conceptual design, business/IT alignment, IT components, and effort.

The layer "*strategic positioning*" covers the purpose of the MSS, *conceptual design* the content needed, as well as the process with which the content is generated. *Business/IT-alignment* covers methods, models, and tools to gain flexibility of the MSS and the *IT components* are covering new IT-enablers such as software and hardware. In terms of the IS' input, the *effort* to design and implement MSS analyses the adequacy of the amount of money and time spent.

In the final step, evaluation criteria are derived from our literature review and complemented by the findings from a manager expert focus group[1] to specify the more general design criteria and make them measurable.

3 Developing the Artefact

3.1 Survey Design and Sample Characteristics

To develop the design guidelines we applied the set of requirements in a multi-case study. *Case studies* are "... applications of an artefact to a real-world situation, evaluating its effect on the real-world situation" [58]. They enable in-depth examination of a topic which is adequate to a complex topic like MSS [59].

We propose a *multi-case study* for our research, obtaining more compelling and robust results across individual cases in contrast to a single-case study [59]. It is also easier to determine appropriate levels of construct abstraction from more than one case [60]. We meet Yin's proposal of about 6–10 cases for a multi-case study with

[1] The manager expert focus group covers heads of management accounting or group BI of large inter-national companies listed in the FT "Europe 500" report (http://www.rcw.wi.tu-darmstadt.de/ccuss).

	Attributes		Case Companies					
General	Company		Company 1	Company 2	Company 3	Company 4	Company 5	Company 6
	Revenue [bn EUR, 2013]		39	60	33	16	74	17
	Employees [thousands, 2013]		161	230	177	47	112	66
	Industry		Raw material and technology	Tele-communication	Automotive and transportation	Manufacturing	Chemical	Software
Monthly Management Report	Number of [recipients]		23	90	60	26	100	7
	Number of [pages]		120	270	230	35	40	30-40
	MMR finished at [working day] every month		16	16	14-16	4	6	15-20
	Covered Information Clusters	Financial Accounting	●	●	●	●	●	●
		Management Accouting	●	●	◑	○	●	●
		Cash Flow & Liquidity Mgmt	●	●	●	●	●	◑
		Program Mgmt	●	*	○	○	●	◑
		Compliance Mgmt	●	*	○	○	*	*
	Advanced Performance Mgmt	Risk Mgmt	●	*	*	*	●	◑
		Environmental Scanning	◕	*	●	◕	◕	◕
		Integrated Exception Reporting	○	○	○	○	○	●
	Used IT-enabler	Mobile Usage Support	○	Webcockpit	○	iPad App	○	iPad App
		Collaboration	○	○	○	○	○	○
		In-Memory Technology	○	◔	○	○	○	◑
		Predictive Analytics on big data	○	◔	○	○	○	◑
	Needed [FTE] for report generation		2 1/2	4	10	2	n/a	8

Harvey balls show coverage of the topic in the respective MMR. An empty harvey ball is a Likert rating of 1 (very low) and a full harvey ball is a Likert rating of 5 (very high).
** Information is provided to the MMR recipients in additional reports, which are not integrated in the MSS.*

Fig. 3 Case company description and excerpt of the multi-case study results

six different companies [59]. They are described in Fig. 3 by revenue, number of employees, industry and an excerpt of the multi-case study results.

Since "selection of an appropriate population [...] helps to define the limits for generalizing the findings" [61], we chose the companies from different industries but with similar size in terms of workforce and revenue. The study was conducted over a period of 6 weeks. We chose semi-structured interviews driven by our set of requirements and complementing observations as data collection method to finally explore best practices and design gaps in existing MSS.

3.2 Multi-Case Study

The representatives of the six case companies are heads of (group) reporting, management accounting, and planning and risk. Two of the four researchers and two company representatives were present at all times during the interviews to reduce subjectivity and ensure a comprehensive documentation of relevant information.

We chose a seven-step approach for data collection[2]: (1) Basic presentation of the MSS by the company's representatives and joint "Q&A" with the researchers to provide a general understanding of the MSS, (2) analysis of the (monthly) top management report and the associated executive summary ("front page"), (3) a semi-structured detailed interview using our criteria list, explaining each EC, and letting the company representatives respond.

[2] This approach is based on suggestions from [59, 61, 62].

The interviews were either on-site or by telephone conference (see Table 1). Furthermore, we received the monthly management report to examine it on-site.[3] (4) The results were discussed afterwards by the researchers and documented in a spreadsheet. (5) This process was followed by one feedback round to discuss open questions with the company's representatives. (6) After all cases were documented they were rated on a 5-point Likert-scale[4] for every EC, where 1 is defined as "not covered or in use" and 5 as "fully covered or leveraged". The rating was done in a discussion by the researchers. (7) This was followed by a presentation of the results in a workshop with all companies. Finally, the rating was discussed and with small adjustments the data collection was finished.

3.3 Develop Design Guidelines

The cross-case analysis exposes either design gaps or "best practices", both listed in Fig. 4. We depict the rating of each company's monthly reporting by each EC, the

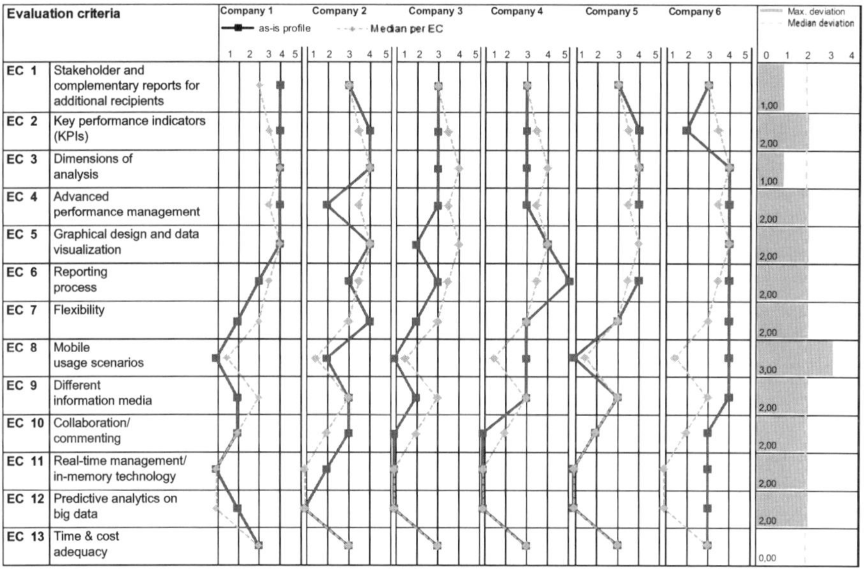

Fig. 4 Ratings of the case companies per EC and deviation analysis

[3] Solely one company denied an insight into their management report due fear of disclosure of its content. Their results are based on their explanation of their MSS.

[4] Since a 5, 7, and 10 Point scale seem to perform roughly equivalent, we chose a 5-point scale because it can easily be represented as Harvey Balls [63].

median over all cases per EC,[5] the maximum deviation per EC, and the median of the deviation to outline the biggest deviations over all ECs. The differences between as-is values and the median values per EC gives an indication towards the positioning of a case within the six cases. The maximum deviation shows the heterogeneity of a single evaluation criterion and is supported by a median over all EC.

More in detail, the median of all cases over all ECs is "3." Looking at the maximum deviation the most values are coincide with the median (2). This shows that there is moderate, but uniformly deviation between the different companies in terms of fulfillment of the particular ECs.

Finding 1 (EC 1): There are different approaches of monthly management reporting. The examined cases vary greatly by scope, extent, and the number of MSS recipients such as quick overview vs. comprehensive reference book.

Because of different reporting scopes, the MSS reports have a heterogeneous volume in terms of number of pages (30–270 pp.) and recipients to be addressed (7–100 people). Except for one case (Company 5), the number of pages is roughly positive correlated to the number of recipients. In this regard the full MSS reports are mostly received by first and second level executives and corporate functions (SVP). Third level executives receive only excerpts specific to their area of responsibility, if any at all. The supervisory board is mostly supplied with an excerpt or summary of the MSS reports.

Design guideline 1
Design MSS as a single point of truth for all relevant stakeholders. Satisfy different information needs by offering a management summary and more detailed analyses of different types such as drill-downs, OLAP analyses and real-time operations.

Finding 2 (EC 2–4, 12): While environmental scanning topics are integrated, the MSS mostly focuses on financial KPIs and fail to include exception reporting as well as additional information sources.

KPIs from financial accounting and cash flow and liquidity management have a strong presence in the MSS reports. The coverage of management accounting, program management, and compliance management are less in the focus of current MSS. They are often reported separately. Methods such as predictive analytics on big data to gain novel insights from new data sources are not leveraged.

[5] This cannot replace an as-is and to-be comparison, but because of the lack of the latter this should be a viable first indication for finding design gaps in today's MSS as well as spotting best practices from already satisfying ECs.

Design guideline 2
Establish MSS as the one-stop-shop by covering most important information clusters including non-financial metrics. Integrate environmental scanning, risk reporting, as well as exception reporting to provide a broad overview over the company's health.

Finding 3 (EC5): While an uncluttered report design is predominately implemented, clear guidance in how to use a report are scarce. Regarding the visualization, there are mostly simple bar and line charts in use.

Looking at the look & feel and understandability, the majority of MSS have recently been redesigned using state of the art design guidelines for effective report design. Therefore most of the redesigned reports meet high standards of quality. Microcharts are seldom used, even though they offer a good overview in a small space. Besides tables, simple bar and line charts are still dominating the reports. The use of indications and highlighting is mixed. Value-driver trees are used in every second company. Only one company uses a dedicated legend page to explain charts and color-coding.

Design guideline 3
Provide a concise look & feel within the MSS through a consistent color-coding. Use indications, highlighting, and advanced charts to expose relevant topics. Have a clear and consistent design concept and enrich pure metrics with graphics. Consider a decomposition of value-driver trees with various KPIs.

Finding 4 (EC8-9): Paper-based reports are the standard reporting medium followed by static electronic documents.

The MSS reports are provided mostly in a static version either on paper or electronic PPT/PDF format. The digital versions usually offer shortcuts to navigate by clicking on information. Native mobile apps are rarely used to cater mobile IS use situations and leverage the capabilities of smart devices. More companies offer web-based user interfaces which are not optimized for mobile devices with smaller screen sizes.

Design guideline 4
Provide a mobile-first MSS on different information media which accommodates the IS use situations of new-generation managers. Caching of information helps to decrease the effect of limited connectivity in "mobile offline" IS use situations.

Finding 5 (EC10): MSS lack modern information media and therefore miss the possibility to leverage collaboration at its full potential.

The extent to which commenting is provided varies greatly from no commenting at all to comments for every significant performance indicator deviation. Due to the lack of interactive media the companies mainly employ management comments by the reporting departments. Company 2 has comments at the level of certain performance indicators and their deviations. Company 3 and 4 either have no commenting at all or provide management comments in different reporting strands. Advanced collaboration features such as interactive commenting and notifications within the MSS are missing altogether. Only Company 2 offers the capability to share contents from within the web application which basically is a shortcut to an email client.

Design guideline 5
Use in-line comments to explain deviations on the most important performance indicators. Features to enable collaboration should be implemented as well to further facilitate self-service MSS use.

4 Demonstrate

4.1 Project Description

To demonstrate utility of our derived design guidelines, a prototype—the new Corporate Navigator app—was developed over 6 months starting in October 2013. It was developed by the authors of this paper with the help of a BI company called MicroStrategy, a vendor for BI software. Based on a software evaluation by Hauke et al. [38], MicroStrategy Analytics Platform [64] in the version 9.3.1 was chosen for its rich selection of visualizations, simple user experience and state of the art mobile capabilities.

On the hardware side, the researchers chose Apple's iPad [65, 66] as tablets strongly increased their market share in comparison to laptops [67].

4.2 The Corporate Navigator Framework

The Corporate Navigator framework and its first instantiation by Marx et al. [11] is based on the St.Gallen Business Engineering framework [57] and consists of *four design layers* comprising strategic positioning, conceptual design, business/IT alignment, and IT components to react flexibly to changing business requirements.

The starting point for the three-step standard reporting is the *Corporate Portfolio* which gives a graphical overview of strategic business units measured by a reward, risk and relevance KPI. The *Corporate Dashboard* exposes in a one-page report format the most important KPIs at a glance, structured by the information clusters financial accounting, management accounting, cash flow- and liquidity management, compliance management, and program management. Information in these clusters can be further analyzed in a final reporting level: the *Corporate Analyses*.

4.3 The Corporate Navigator App

Reworking the Corporate Navigator prototype we have chosen a *mobile-first approach* with the iPad as end-user device. Following our design guidelines, we focused on a self-service design. The specifications were implemented by the BI engineer in an agile approach where all features for the day were defined in the morning, implemented during the day and finally reviewed by the researchers at the end of the day to ensure a good problem fit. A high-level overview of the specifications clustered by the design criteria are depicted in Table 2.

Table 2 Mapping between the design criteria, the specification of the prototype and contributing design guidelines

Design criteria		Specification of the corporate navigator app	Contributing design guidelines
Strategic positioning (WHAT)	Purpose	Three layers of analysis ranging from an overview with the three most important KPIs to fine-grained reports and detailed analyses A digital management folder would provide ancillary information	1
Conceptual design (HOW)	Content	Leveraging non-financial KPIs by providing information from all five information clusters in dashboards and analyses Provide the manager with exception reports to inform about critical issues	2
	Visualization	Consistent color coding by highlighting actual KPIs which performed worse, all other KPIs remain black. Provide a view for simulations with a value-driver tree Sparklines leverage their potential on the Corporate Dashboard by providing a temporal context for actual values	3
IT components (WHAT WITH)	New IT-enablers	As an easy-to-use app on an Apple iPad the self-service MSS assists managers even when they are mobile and complements other information channels Besides viewing comments for each KPI, topic or general matter, they can be composed by the managers to foster collaboration	2, 4, 5

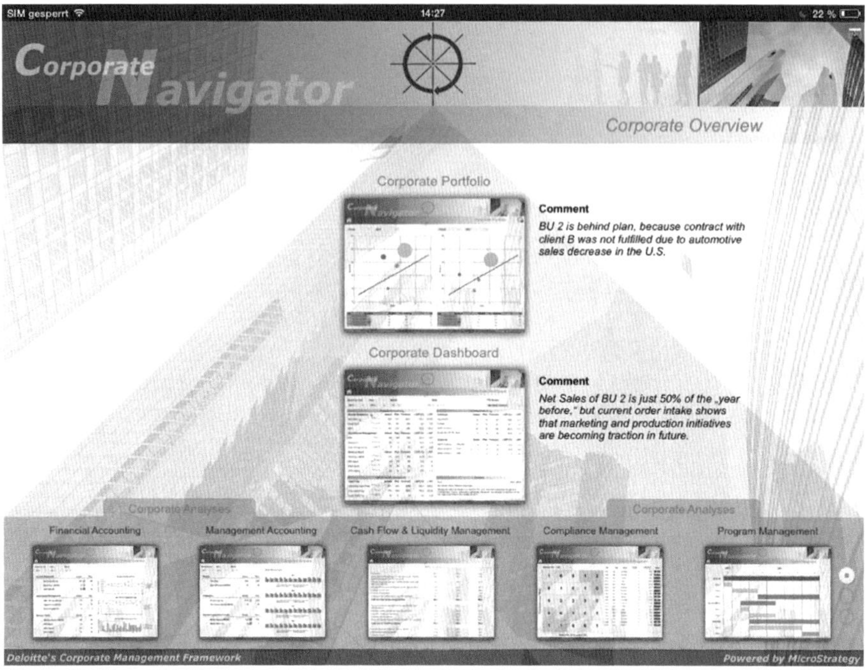

Fig. 5 The corporate overview

Two of the specifications above are supported by MicroStrategy's analytics platform out of the box. Firstly, the platform synchronizes data between the server and the device whenever there is client/server connectivity. In the case the tablet has no connection to the server, data are cached in the MicroStrategy app and can still be displayed to support mobile online and offline use scenarios for managers.

Secondly, exception reports can be pushed to end-user devices as notifications. They include a description and a link to the most relevant report within the app. The manager can then follow the link and analyze the issue or make comments. Automatic notifications can also be received by subscribing KPIs or reports.

Other specifications are implemented within the analytics platform which follow the three-layered reporting structure. The *Corporate Overview* gives an overview and access to the three reporting levels of the Corporate Navigator (Fig. 5).

Comments next to the two important entry points—the Corporate Portfolio and the Corporate Dashboard—give the user guidance to navigate. In the bottom Sect. 5 Corporate Analyses views are visible. They are shown by default but further analyses such as a value-driver tree and geo maps are accessible by swiping to the left. Ancillary information which are provided in the form of PDF, audio or video can be accessed through a management folder.

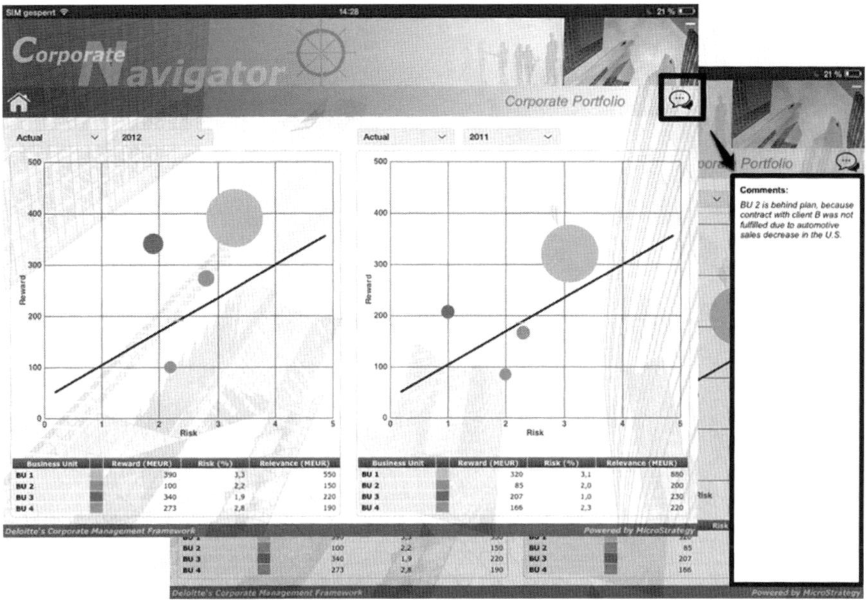

Fig. 6 The corporate portfolio with collaboration bar

Starting a "typical" path of analysis, the *Corporate Portfolio* plays an important role. EBIT (earnings before interest and taxes), EBIT deviation and capital employed were selected as the most important KPIs for a reward, risk and relevance perspective on the companies' strategic business units (SBU). For collaboration a retractable toolbar was implemented. This bar is designed to follow the concept of "show more" and thus is only visible on demand, by taping on the commenting icon (see Fig. 6). By selecting a SBU in the table can navigate to the SBU's Corporate Dashboard.

The Corporate Dashboard (see Fig. 7) consists of five information clusters: financial accounting, management accounting, cash flow & liquidity management as well as compliance and program management, the latter covers an overview of most important projects.

As proposed in the design guidelines a forward-oriented perspective with actual, plan, and forecast replaces the traditional view of past, actual, and plan [11]. Sparklines are used to expose the general trend from the last 12 months. As a result from the expert focus group, deviations from actual and plan values were preferred over actual and forecast as well as plan and forecast. To quickly grasp the year-over-year growth the deviations are shown as absolute and relative values. Negative deviations of the actual values from the plan values result in a highlighting of actual values in red to guide attention towards important deviations (color-coding). The navigation concept includes the use of touch input gestures to switch between a monthly perspective and an aggregated year to date (YTD) perspective by swiping left and right over the whole screen. While a monthly perspective only

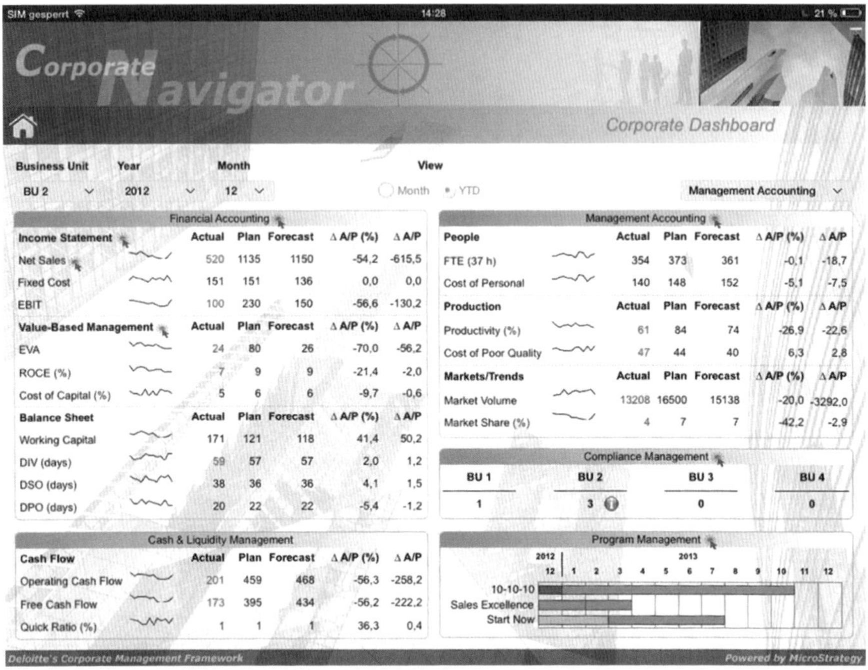

Fig. 7 The corporate dashboard

shows data points from the selected month, the YTD perspective aggregates the data points beginning in January of the selected year to the selected year month.

Links to more detailed analyses such as an Income Statement and Financial Accounting analysis; see Fig. 10 for more) which result in a transition to other views are distinguished with a cursor icon while analyses in the same view can be accessed through swipe gestures on dedicated areas. For instance by swiping the Management Accounting tile, net sales from the Financial Accounting on the left side can be examined more in detail on the right side (see Fig. 8). The analysis comprises a breakdown of net sales by region as well as customers and provides the option to leave comments.

Commenting at a KPI-level is supported in two ways. In both ways it shows contextual information on demand but either in a dedicated area in the screen (left, Fig. 9) or in a popup window (right, Fig. 9). Notification icons informing about further comments can be positioned freely throughout the interface and expose more information as soon as they are activated by a tap.

The *Corporate Analyses* add a third and final layer to the MSS. In Fig. 10 an overview of the analyses is given. All of the analyses serve a special purpose and the design is consistent following the derived design guidelines.

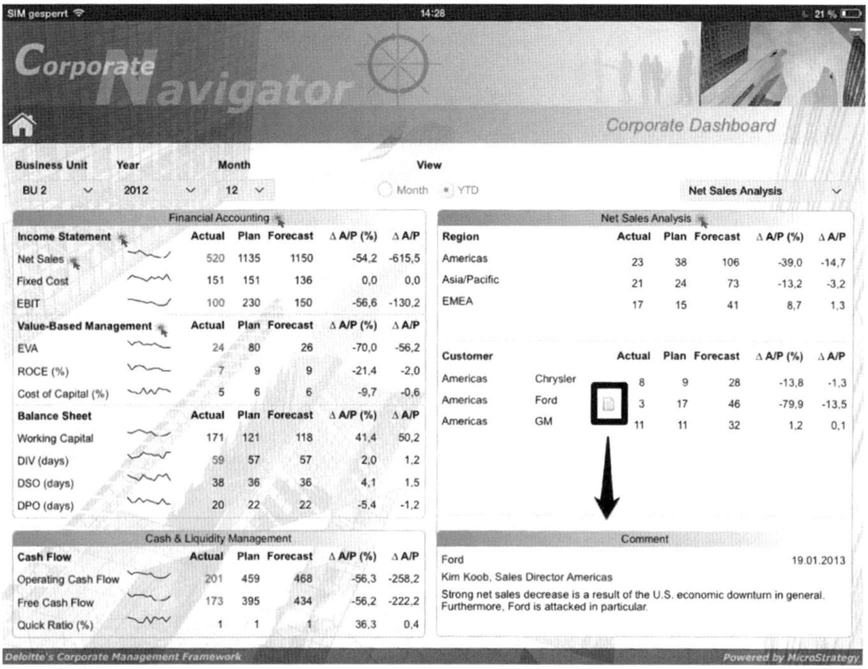

Fig. 8 The corporate dashboard with net sales analysis

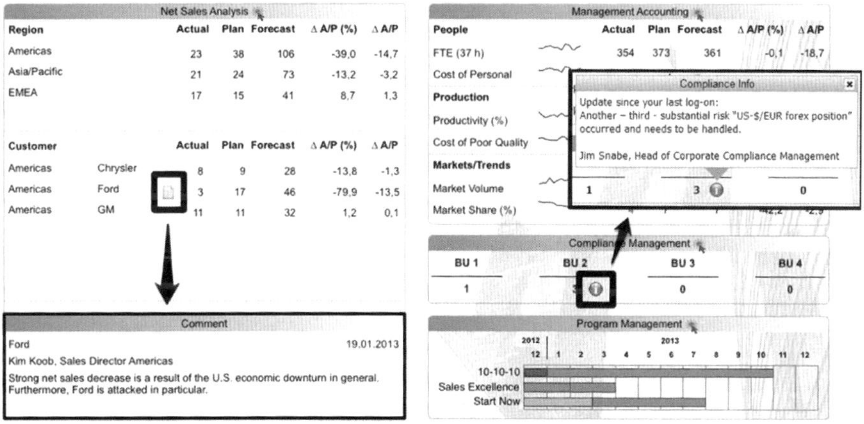

Fig. 9 Commenting at the KPI in the net sales analysis and compliance management

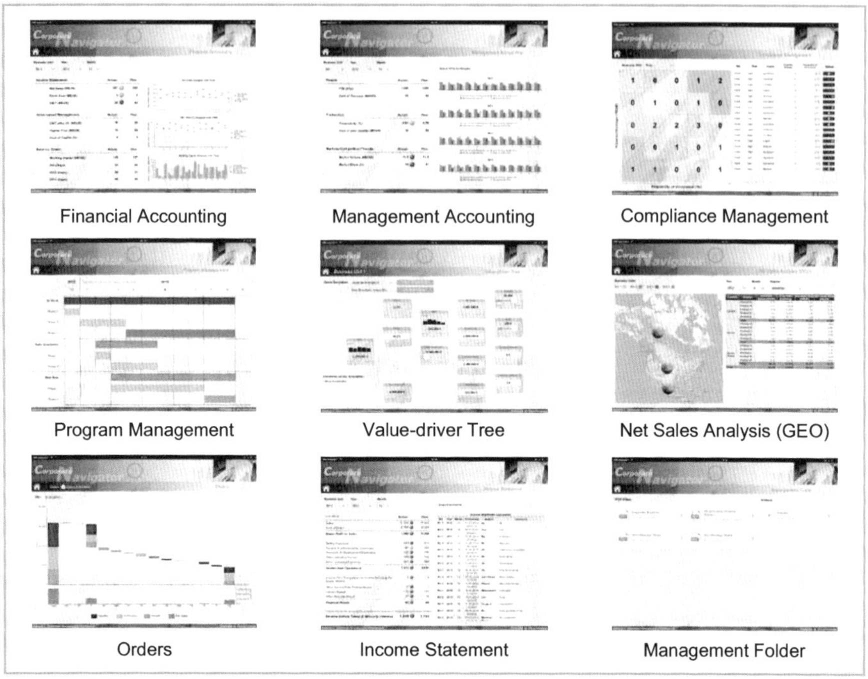

Fig. 10 The corporate analyses and management folder

5 Evaluation

Evaluation in the DSR in IS process has to „observe and measure how well the artefact supports a solution to the problem" [23]. Complementing such *utility*, we evaluate the rigorousness of the DSR in IS process on hand [68].

Since this work is part of a greater project in which the set of requirements were already evaluated [21], this section focuses on the ex-post evaluation of the design guidelines developed in this article. The evaluation took place in a naturalistic context which involves the interaction of real users with real IS to solve real problems [69]. We did the evaluation by interviewing two heads of corporate (group) reporting departments from German DAX companies. Both companies participated in our multi-case study.

The prototype was demonstrated in a semi-structured interview guided by the set of requirements developed before (see Table 1). The answers were qualitative. During the interview two authors of this paper rated the Corporate Navigator app in accordance to managers' assessments. The results from this process give an understanding of how well the design guidelines address the findings we identified in current MSS design and are summarized in Fig. 11.

The managers considered the condensed Corporate Portfolio and Corporate Dashboard design together with the flexibility of the Corporate Analyses as a

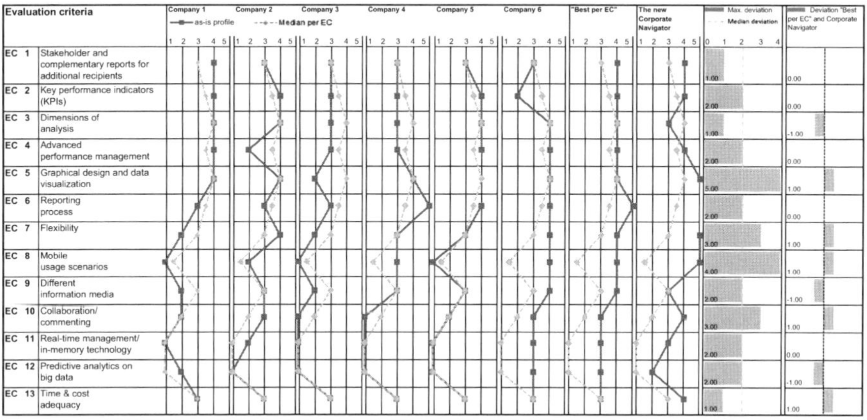

Fig. 11 Comparing the corporate navigator app with existing MSS

unique value proposition of the Corporate Navigator app. In combination with the management folder this MSS app can serve as a single point of information for new-generation managers. Due to the smaller screen on tablets and enlarged controls, there is less space left for more *dimensions of analysis* in reports. Thus, interviewees perceived the capabilities in this area as inferior to top class.

However, a balanced relationship between *financials and non-financials* through the five information cluster resulted in an on par rating with the leading companies examined in the case study. By its incorporation, risk management, value-driver tree and environmental scanning, the *advanced performance management* convinced the managers as well. Only the driver tree showed room for improvement since it (a) assumes a single product company which is not often the case and (b) should offer more options to drill down on performance indicators.

The top ranking in the *graphical design and data visualization* arises from two factors. Firstly, a high usability is the result of a design adapted to the specifics of the information medium (i.e., app on a tablet) in combination with an intuitive navigation. Secondly, advanced visualizations such as sparklines, waterfall charts and geo maps contribute to an improved "look&feel" and lever their strengths especially in the restricted screen estate of a tablet.

Since delays in the *reporting process* are not the result of technical issues but organizational inefficiencies the Corporate Navigator app could not made improvements. This leads us to the conclusion that a rating here is not feasible.

The Corporate Navigator's *flexibility* is driven by the Corporate Analyses in which new reports can be seamlessly integrated. In addition, reports which shall be provided to stakeholders on a short notice can be viewed from the management folder within the app. Through the mobile-first approach *mobile use scenarios* are perfectly supported by the Corporate Navigator app, but lack the capability to export the information to further *information media* such as PDF or paper. To support the latter a print feature is needed.

Collaboration (mainly commenting) was appreciated by the managers as well since it is substantial to give a clear picture of the company's current situation and provide contextual information. Although, other IT-enablers such as *in-memory technologies* and *predictive analytics* are used in the Corporate Navigator app and their benefits has been acknowledged by the managers, the full potential has not been leveraged yet. Therefore the rating is limited in both criteria.

A strength of the predefined Corporate Navigator framework is resource efficiency. The project team needed just 21 man-days to implement the current state of the app and therefore undercuts the average implementation length strongly. Thus, the *cost effectiveness* is higher than in other custom implementations.

Overall the Corporate Navigator app represents significant progress towards self-service MSS to support new-generation managers and their multifaceted work.

6 Conclusion and Avenues for Future Research

The work at hand completes a greater research project[6] in self-service MSS for new-generation managers leveraging new IT-enablers. A set of requirements for self-service MSS was taken from prior research [21]. These requirements were used to evaluate six MSS of German DAX companies in a multi-case study. Based on the case study's findings, design guidelines for self-service MSS were derived and, then, evaluated by a mobile-first prototype: the Corporate Navigator app. To demonstrate progress in research an evaluation of the prototype with two companies from the multi-case study was conducted.

There are several limitations which lead to the following avenues for future research: Firstly, even if the principle of economic efficiency is well-proven, the *cost and time* to develop the MSS accessed in the case study could not be measured. This was a problem of confidentiality and amount of work put into quantifying the effort needed to build and operate the MSS by the case companies, rather than a fundamental flaw in the artefact or its demonstration itself. Future research should focus on obtaining a rating in this criterion.

Secondly, the lack of a *to-be profile* is a more serious limitation of this work. A first step towards developing a to-be profile could be that managers rate their satisfaction with the different aspects (e.g., on the evaluation or design criteria level) and their appeal towards self-service use of MSS.

Thirdly, the five design guidelines on hand can serve as recommendations to design self-service MSS with a focus on management reporting. However, our case study is only a *first snapshot*. We propose to observe the continuous validity of the guidelines. This may be of interest due to changes in user requirements and emergence of other IT-enablers. Future research should keep social and technical progress in mind as well.

---

[6] [21, 24, 70, 71].

Fourthly, the design guidelines were evaluated by heads of corporate (group) reporting departments, thus it remains unknown how the *board of directors* would have evaluated the prototype.

Another avenue for future research could be the implication of ubiquitous information access through self-service MSS. The constant engagement with ICT (e.g., smart devices) creates so called *technostress* [72]. Thus future research could examine the effects of self-service MSS on the individual manager as well. This could lead to further design guidelines from a non-technical direction.

References

1. Johnson G, Scholes K, Whittington R (2008) Exploring corporate strategy. Financial times. Prentice Hall, London
2. Porter ME (1996) What is strategy? Harv Bus Rev 74(6):61–78
3. Ackoff RL (1967) Management misinformation systems. Manag Sci 14(4):147–156
4. Mintzberg H (1972) The myths of MIS. Calif Manag Rev XV(1):92–97
5. Rockart JF, Treacy ME (1989) The CEO goes on-line. In: Nelson RR (ed) End-user computing: concepts, issues, and applications. Wiley, New York, pp 55–64
6. Leidner DE, Elam JJ (1993) Executive information systems: their impact on executive decision making. J Manag Inf Syst 10(3):139
7. Wixom BH, Watson HJ (2010) The BI-based organization. Int J Bus Intell Res 1(1):13–28
8. Carlsson SA, Henningsson S, Hrastinski S, Keller C (2009) An approach for designing management support systems: the design science research process and its outcomes. In: Baskerville R, Purao S (eds) Vaishanvi V. Proceedings of the fourth international conference on design science research in information systems and technology, Malvern, pp 1–10
9. Watson HJ (2009) Tutorial: business intelligence - past, present, and future. Commun AIS 2009(25):487–510
10. Eckerson WW (2010) Transforming finance: how CFOs use business intelligence to turn finance from record keepers to strategic advisors. TDWI, Renton
11. Marx F, Mayer JH, Winter R (2011) Six principles for redesigning executive information systems—findings of a survey and evaluation of a prototype. ACM Transac Manag Inf Syst 2 (4):26
12. Vodanovich S, Sundaram D, Myers M (2010) Digital natives and ubiquitous information systems. Inf Syst Res 21(4):711–723
13. McGrath RG (2013) Transient advantage. Harv Bus Rev 91(6):62–70
14. Mayer JH, Winter R, Mohr T (2012) Situational management support systems. Bus Inf Syst Eng 4(6):331–345
15. Tengblad S (2006) Is there a 'new managerial work'? A comparison with Henry Mintzberg's classic study 30 years later. J Manag Stud 43(7):1437–1461
16. Meuter ML, Ostrom AL, Roundtree RI, Bitner MJ (2000) Self-service technologies: understanding customer satisfaction with technology-based service encounters. J Mark 64(3):50–64
17. Mayer JH (2013) Current changes in executive work and how to handle them by redesigning executive information systems. In: Mancini D, Vaassen E, Dameri RP (eds) Accounting information systems for decision making, vol 3, LNISO. Springer, Heidelberg, pp 134–155
18. Stodder D (2013) Achieving greater agility with business intelligence: improving speed and flexibility for BI, analytics, and data warehousing. TDWI Research, Renton
19. Plattner H, Zeier A (2011) In-memory data management. Springer, Heidelberg
20. Puuronen S, Savolainen V (1997) Mobile information systems—executives' view. Inf Syst J 7 (1):3–20

21. Mayer JH, Röder A, Hartwig J, Quick R (2014) A self-service MSS design from a new-generation manager perspective. In: Tremblay M, VanderMeer D, Rothenberger M, Gupta A, Yoon V (eds) Advancing the impact of design science: moving from theory to practice (DESRIST 2014), vol 8463, Lecture notes in computer science. Springer, Berlin, pp 164–179
22. Hevner AR, Chatterjee S (2010) Design science research in information systems. In: Design research in information systems. Springer, New York, pp 9–22
23. Peffers K, Tuunanen T, Gengler CE, Rossi M, Hui W, Virtanen V, Bragge J (2006) The design science research process: a model for producing and presenting information systems research. In: Chatterjee S, Hevner A (eds) 1st international conference on design science in information systems and technology, Claremont, pp 83–106, 24 Feb 2006
24. Mayer JH, Koschtial C, Hartwig J, Röder A (2014) Corporate navigator app–a new-generation management support system. In: Advancing the impact of design science: moving from theory to practice (DESRIST 2014). Springer, Berlin, pp 423–427
25. vom Brocke J, Simons A, Niehaves B, Riemer K, Plattfaut R, Cleven A (2009) Reconstructing the giant: on the importance of rigour in documenting the literature search process. In: Newell S, Whitley E, Pouloudi N, Wareham J, Mathiassen L (eds) 17th European conference on information systems (ECIS). Verona, pp 2206–2217
26. Willcocks LP, Whitley EA, Avgerou C (2008) The ranking of top IS journals: a perspective from the London school of economics. Eur J Inf Syst 17(2):163–168
27. Tricker B (1997) Editorial: what information do directors really need? Corp Govern Int Rev 5 (3):109–111
28. Aders C, Hebertinger M, Schaffer C, Wiedemann F (2003) Shareholder Value-Konzepte–Umsetzung bei den DAX100-Unternehmen. Finanz Betrieb 5(11):719–725
29. Cheung W, Babin G (2006) A metadatabase-enabled executive information system (Part B): methods for dynamic multidimensional data analysis. Decis Support Syst 42(3):1599–1612
30. Ghazanfari M, Jafari M, Rouhani S (2011) A tool to evaluate the business intelligence of enterprise systems. Sci Iran 18(6):1579–1590
31. Houdeshel G, Watson HJ (1987) The management information and decision support (MIDS) system at Lockheed-Georgia. MIS Q 11(1):127–140
32. Marx F, Wortmann F, Mayer JH (2012) A maturity model for management control systems - five evolutionary steps to guide development. Bus Inf Syst Eng 4(4):193–207
33. Işık Ö, Jones MC, Sidorova A (2013) Business intelligence success: the roles of BI capabilities and decision environments. Inf Manag 50(1):13–23
34. Armstrong SJ, Cools E, Sadler-Smith E (2012) Role of cognitive styles in business and management: reviewing 40 years of research. Int J Manag Rev 14(3):238–262
35. DeFond ML, Francis JR (2005) Audit research after sarbanes-oxley. Auditing J Pract Theory 24(S–1):5–30
36. Axson DAJ (2007) Best practices in planning and performance management: from data to decisions. Wiley, New York
37. Galloway DL (2010) Achieving accurate metrics using balanced scorecards and dashboards. Perform Improv 49(7):38–45
38. Hauke J, Mayer JH, Quick R, Feistenauer H (2013) New-generation managers' business/IT alignment perspective for a more business-driven is design. In: Abramowicz W (ed) Business information systems workshops, vol 160, Lecture notes in business information processing. Springer, Berlin, pp 73–88
39. Dutta S, Wierenga B, Dalebout A (1997) Designing management support systems using an integrative perspective. Commun ACM 40(6):70–79
40. Sharma AK, Kumar S (2010) Economic value added (EVA)-literature review and relevant issues. Int J Econ Financ 2(2)
41. Wu J (2005) Harnessing the power of exception reporting. DM Rev 15(9):16–68
42. Houghton R, El Sawy O, Gray P, Donegan C, Joshi A (2004) Vigilant information systems for managing enterprises in dynamic supply chains: real-time dashboards at western digital. MIS Q Exec 3(1):19–35

43. Few S (2006) Information dashboard design: the effective visual communication of data, 1st edn. O'Reilly Media, Cambridge
44. Yigitbasioglu OM, Velcu O (2012) A review of dashboards in performance management: implications for design and research. Int J Account Inf Syst 13(1):41–59
45. Pijpers GGM, Bemelmans TMA, Heemstra FJ, van Montfort KAGM (2001) Senior executives' use of information technology. Inf Softw Technol 43(15):959–971
46. Andersson B, Henningsson S (2010) Developing mobile information systems: managing additional aspects. In: ECIS 2010 proceedings, 2010. Paper 2
47. Mayer JH, Bischoff S, Winter R, Weitzel T (2012) Extending traditional EIS use to support mobile executives online and offline. MIS Q Exec 11(2):87–96
48. Lawson R, Desroches D, Hatch T (2008) Scorecard best practices: design, implementation, and evaluation. Wiley, Hoboken
49. Parr Rud O (2009) Business intelligence success factors: tools for aligning your business in the global economy, 1st edn. Wiley, Hoboken
50. Shim JP, Warkentin M, Courtney JF, Power DJ, Sharda R, Carlsson C (2002) Past, present, and future of decision support technology. Decis Support Syst 33(2):111–126
51. Demirkan H, Delen D (2013) Leveraging the capabilities of service-oriented decision support systems: putting analytics and big data in cloud. Decis Support Syst 55(1):412–421
52. Watson HJ, Wixom BH, Hoffer JA, Anderson-Lehman R, Reynolds AM (2006) Real-time business intelligence: best practices at continental airlines. Inf Syst Manag 23(1):7–18
53. Nemati HR, Steiger DM, Iyer LS, Herschel RT (2002) Knowledge warehouse: an architectural integration of knowledge management, decision support, artificial intelligence and data warehousing. Decis Support Syst 33(2):143–161
54. Schober F, Gebauer J (2011) How much to spend on flexibility? Determining the value of information system flexibility. Decis Support Syst 51(3):638–647
55. Charles TH (1995) Regular article: management accounting: this century and beyond. Manag Account Res 6:281–286
56. Samuelson PA (1983) Foundations of economic analysis, 1st edn. Harvard University Press, Cambridge
57. Österle H, Blessing D (2003) Business engineering modell. In: Business engineering. Springer, Heidelberg, pp 65–85
58. Peffers K, Rothenberger M, Tuunanen T, Vaezi R (2012) Design science research evaluation. In: Design science research in information systems. Advances in theory and practice (DESRIST 2012). Springer, Berlin, pp 398–410
59. Yin RK (2009) Case study research: design and methods. Sage, Thousand Oaks
60. Eisenhardt KM, Graebner ME (2007) Theory building from cases: opportunities and challenges. Acad Manag J 50(1):25–32
61. Eisenhardt KM (1989) Building theories from case study research. Acad Manag Rev 14 (4):532–550
62. Bourgeois LJ III, Eisenhardt KM (1988) Strategic decision processes in high velocity environments: four cases in the microcomputer industry. Manag Sci 34(7):816–835
63. Dawes J (2008) Do data characteristics change according to the number of scale points used? An experiment using 5 point, 7 point and 10 point scales. Int J Mark Res 51(1)
64. MicroStrategy Inc (2014) MicroStrategy analytics platform. MicroStrategy Inc. http://www.microstrategy.com/us/platforms/analytics/overview. Accessed Oct 10 2014
65. Apple Inc (2014) iPad in business. Apple Inc. https://www.apple.com/ipad/business/it/security. html. Accessed 10 Oct 2014
66. TechTarget (2014) Apple enterprise features for managing iOS devices. TechTarget. http://searchconsumerization.techtarget.com/essentialguide/Apple-enterprise-features-for-managing-iOS-devices. Accessed 10 Oct 2014
67. International Data Corporation (2013) Tablet shipments forecast to top total PC shipments in the fourth quarter of 2013 and annually by 2015. According to IDC International Data Corporation (IDC). http://www.idc.com/getdoc.jsp?containerId=prUS24314413. Accessed 01 Dec 2014

68. Hevner AR, March ST, Park J, Ram S (2004) Design science in information systems research. MIS Q 28(1):75–105
69. Venable J, Pries-Heje J, Baskerville R (2012) A comprehensive framework for evaluation in design science research. In: Design science research in information systems. Advances in theory and practice. Springer, Berlin, pp 423–438
70. Hartwig J (2014) Designing a self-service management support system frontend from a managers perspective. Studienarbeit, Darmstadt University of Technology, Darmstadt
71. Röder A (2014) Designing a business-driven self-service management support system for new-generation managers. Studienarbeit, Darmstadt University of Technology, Darmstadt
72. Ayyagari R, Grover V, Purvis R (2011) Technostress: technological antecedents and implications. MIS Q 35(4):831–858